The Write Start

the write start

A Guide to Nurturing Writing at Every Stage,
from Scribbling to Forming Letters and Writing Stories

JENNIFER HALLISSY

ROOST
BOOKS

Boston & London || 2010

Roost Books
An imprint of Shambhala Publications, Inc.
Horticultural Hall
300 Massachusetts Avenue
Boston, Massachusetts 02115
roostbooks.com

9 8 7 6 5 4 3 2

Printed in the United States of America

♼This edition is printed on acid-free paper that meets the American National Standards Institute z39.48 Standard.
♻Shambhala Publications makes every effort to print on recycled paper.
For more information please visit www.shambhala.com

Distributed in the United States by Random House, Inc.,
and in Canada by Random House of Canada Ltd

Designed by Daniel Urban-Brown

Library of Congress Cataloging-in-Publication Data
Hallissy, Jennifer.
The write start: a guide to nurturing writing at every stage, from scribbling to forming letters and writing stories / Jennifer Hallissy.—1st ed.
p. cm.
Includes bibliographical references.
ISBN 978-1-59030-837-0 (pbk.: alk. paper) 1. Children—Writing. 2. Children—Language. 3. Child development. I. Title.
LB1139.W7H35 2010
372.62'3—dc22
2010023070

To Bruce,
who built me the life of my dreams.

and to Jack and Gracie,
my dreams come true.

Contents

52 "Just Write" Activities

Learn

Connect

Acknowledgments

MY PROFOUND appreciation goes to my editor, Jennifer Urban-Brown, and everyone at Roost Books, for embracing a little book about learning to write, right from the start.

Thank you to my parents, who started it all.

To my mother, who (among many other things) taught me to write. She also served as a proofreader, consultant, and writing role model. Most of all, returning a favor, her confidence in me shamed me into completing this book.

To my father, who (among many other things) taught me to fish. Although seemingly unrelated, the many hours we spent honing the art of baiting hooks, casting out, waiting patiently, untangling lines, and having faith prepared me for the craft of writing a book (and for life). Though we never caught much, I sure learned plenty.

Thank you to everyone else, who kept me going.

To my sisters, Maria and Megan, who are relentlessly supportive and have never let me down.

To my dear friend Regina Bast, who listens to my chatter and tolerates my quiet with incomparable grace and understanding.

To Elizabeth Eskanasi and Rya Levin, my first readers (and cheerleaders). To Renee Lockhart, whose persistent question, "How can we be most effective?" has become my touchstone. To Nora Strecker, who shares gentle wisdom on publishing, parenting, and life. To Allison Gillis of *Wondertime,* for graciously initiating me into the real world of writing. To Christina Katz, who provided pitch-perfect advice. To the online community of bloggers and blog readers, some of the most intelligent and creative people I've never met. And to all the children I've worked with, who have been my wisest teachers.

I give thanks *and* my heart to my children, my reason to be. To my son, Jack, who has been with me every step of the way, learning with me, inspiring me, and harboring unwavering faith in me. And to Gracie, for devoted lap warming and back patting (while also nursing her own editorial aspirations by marking up my manuscript and reorganizing my pages).

Above all, I thank my husband, Bruce, without whom, nothing.

The Write Start

Introduction
From Scribbles to Script

MY INTEREST IN TEACHING parents about writing-skill development started, like many things do, as a burning desire to solve a problem. As a young, go-getting occupational therapist, I consistently had a full caseload (and ever-growing waiting list) of children ranging in age from preschool to middle school. All of these children qualified for occupational therapy services, meaning that they demonstrated some measurable delay in their ability to perform age-appropriate developmental tasks. As a pediatric occupational therapist, it is *my* daily job to help kids master the skills they need to be successful at all of *their* daily jobs. To accomplish this, I do my best to combine everything I know about the science of child development with the art of creating the just-right activity for each child's individual needs.

I was an itinerant therapist, which meant I traveled all around the neighborhood to see kids in their various environments, including home, school, and clinic settings. I had a car full of toys and tools, and lugged a giant tote full of gear into each appointment. The specific issues each child was experiencing varied. Yet one thing remained consistent across the board: every child I saw struggled with writing. Their teachers knew it, their parents knew it, and, most important, they knew it. From preschoolers who struggled to scribble, to middle schoolers who struggled with script, writing problems were plentiful. And although I loved every minute of working with these kids, a nagging question followed me to each stop. Why are there so many reluctant writers?

Every day as I worked, the question resurfaced. When it comes to teaching these kids to write, where have we gone wrong? Slowly but surely answers emerged. They showed up in the trunk of my car, in my tote, and in my treatment activities themselves. From preschoolers to preteens, all of my kids would consistently gravitate to the same stuff. How could that be? Despite my never-ending bag of tricks and all my cleverly conceived activities, reluctant writers of all ages continued to want (and need) to go back to the basics.

So with all of my reluctant writers, big and little, we went back to the foundation. Foundational skills, that is. Both young and not-so-young kids were on the same page with me as we revisited pre-writing skills. How to hold a pencil. How to sit upright in a chair. How to use one hand as a stabilizer while the other is at work. How to memorize the movements that make up each letter of the alphabet. We worked on hand strengthening, postural control, and eye-hand coordination. We even got down on the floor, crawling, to build shoulder stability, literally approaching the task of writing from the ground up.

And as we focused on the skills that support writing, a funny thing happened. My reluctant writers actually *wanted* to write. And, oh, the stories that came out! All of a sudden there were jokes and silly signs, letters to grandparents, love notes to Mom, diagrams for Daddy, and essays for school. When they began to crack the code of writing, it was as if they had gained a whole new voice, and a wealth of ideas to go along with it. Not to mention the confidence that comes along with mastery.

Now the concept of establishing a strong foundation was something I could really wrap my head around. As the daughter of an architect, this is something that was impressed upon me from a young age. I'll never forget the day when my dad came to my kindergarten class for career day (wearing his hard hat and carrying a set of blueprints) and asked the class the all-important question, "What's the *first* thing you need to build a house?" All of us wannabe builders promptly called out: "A hammer!" "Nails!" "Wood!" "Walls!" "Windows!" "A door!" "A roof!" But one boy sat quietly, hand raised high, and waited for my dad to call on him. "A hole," he said with conviction. And although the children broke out in laughter, my father beamed.

"Yes, John," he nodded approvingly, "to build a house you must start with a hole."

Child development is much like the house that emerges from the hole. Higher-level skills (like writing) need to be built on a strong foundation of basic skills. Lay the groundwork, and development can progress unencumbered. Proceed without proper support, however, and what follows will be shaky, at best.

Armed with this insight, it became my personal mission to catch kids *before* they fell. My goal was to spread the word to parents about writing development, starting with the foundational skills and working my way up. I led workshops, wrote handouts and newsletters, and provided parent consultations. As I now had children of my own, I was able to road test activities at home. Becoming a parent afforded me the additional insight that if something isn't easy to incorporate into the daily routine, it won't get done. So I learned how to serve up some writing readiness at mealtimes, pack it into car trips, tuck it into the bedtime routine, and wrap it up in holiday rituals. Because I am conscious of the developmental importance of writing, adding it to the daily grind has become second nature to me. And like most parents, I am juggling *a lot*. So I assure you, if I can do it with very little fuss, I know that you can too.

The Write Idea

So when does writing start and why? From the first time your baby swipes carrot puree across the high chair tray, then catches your eye as if to say, "Look what I did!" to scribbling, drawing, making squiggles, symbols, and letters, inventing spellings and words, noting numbers, creating tally marks, diagrams, you name it, your child is writing. Writing is making marks that have meaning. Since children are naturally creative, they will come up with all sorts of inventive ways to communicate or document their thoughts by using whatever marks they are able to make. All are valid, and all should be valued.

Learning to write is a milestone of childhood, one that ranks right up there with baby's first smile, first steps, and first words. What these momentous events have in common is self-expression. Each of these events propels a child from passive to active, from thinking to doing. Writing is thought in action. It is one of the fundamental ways a child communicates to the world,

"Hey! This is what's on my mind." When you reinforce all your children's attempts at writing—even those scribbles and squiggles—you help them learn that they can communicate effectively using this fascinating medium.

Children, like all humans, have an inherent need to express themselves. They are innately interested in finding the means and methods to record and communicate their ideas. From their first crude marks onward, their writings reflect this uniquely human desire to say "I am here" and "This is my story."

And, although helping your children to achieve the writing skills that enable them to share their thoughts, feelings, and desires is a hugely worthwhile task on its own, the benefits of raising a writer go way beyond that. Writing allows us to do so much more than express ourselves—it's an essential tool we use every day for a variety of practical (and productive) reasons.

Strong writing skills are inextricably linked with children's lifelong learning, literacy, and academic and employment success. More than ever, in this "age of information," children need to take ownership of all the knowledge surrounding them. And writing remains the very best way to do that.

The Link to Learning

Thinking and learning are not one and the same. Thinking is a passive pursuit; learning is active. In order for learning to occur, there has to be an active expression of thought. Writing is self-expression at its most active. It is the tool by which we communicate what we have understood. Through the process of writing, children integrate knowledge and make it their own. This is the very definition of learning.

The Link to Literacy

Good writers make great readers. Why? Because practicing letter formation when writing reinforces speedy letter recognition when reading. Writing also reinforces important left-to-right and top-to-bottom concepts inherent to reading. Most of all, writing gives children a tool to build words and stories from the sounds they already know. This emerging ability to write down their thoughts lays the foundation for children's desire to read the thoughts and ideas of others.

You may be surprised to learn that, for developing children, writing often precedes reading. How can this be? Because writing, like spoken language, is self-generated. Once children are able to link sounds to letters, they are ready to write their own thoughts and then read them back to themselves. And children who are able to read their own writing are well-equipped to read the writing of others. Better yet, children who learn to read their own writing first expend less effort decoding when reading, which frees up more of their attentional resources to focus on meaning.

The Link to Academic Success

Good writers also make great students. The speed and ease of children's writing can have a major impact on their overall academic success. Time and again it has been found that children who are able to write quickly and automatically outperform their peers across the curriculum.

The ability to write well is consistently related to academic success, both in research and in reality. And by "good writing" we don't mean perfect copybook penmanship either. Effective writing should be legible—both to the writer and the reader. But, even more important, effective writing should be efficient. Efficient writing flows quickly and easily from the hand of the writer. It is natural, almost effortless. Efficient writers' pencils are able to keep up with their thoughts. A pencil that moves freely and easily is a vehicle for self-expression, communication, and learning. And, apparently, an efficient pencil can write a child's ticket to academic success.

Efficient writers have an edge on their peers when it comes to note taking, homework, and studying for tests. This holds true in every subject young students encounter across the board. Whether in a science, math, history, or language class, students need to be able to record, relay, and review information quickly and easily through writing in order to learn. And when it comes to testing, it is not surprising that students who write faster consistently achieve higher grades on written exams.

Efficient writers have another less obvious advantage over their classmates: a greater ability to pay attention. Since efficient writers don't have to focus their attention on the mechanics of writing, they are able to focus on what really matters—meaning. Making meaningful connections is what academic learning is all about. Students who write with ease are able to devote all of their attentional resources to the meaning of the written words. This attention is the basis for comprehension.

It doesn't end there. Efficient writers surpass their peers in productivity in school as well. Simply stated, the better children are at writing, the more they will write. And the more they write, the better they will get at writing. As their writing improves, their learning is enhanced, as is their performance across the curriculum. Not to mention their confidence and self-esteem, the immeasurable fringe benefits of academic success.

The Link to Higher Education

When most high schoolers and their parents begin contemplating college, they shudder at the thought of the ubiquitous college essay. High school guidance counselors begin planting the seeds early on, assuring everyone that a knockout essay can open many doors for a student. As it turns out, the college essay is just the first of many writing challenges in store for college students.

The writing on the ivy walls is clear: good writing is the cornerstone of higher education. Solid writing skills provide a strong foundation for students who aspire to succeed in college. And a love of writing learned early on will certainly make it easier for children to choose the path that leads to a university education.

College courses take writing to a whole new level. No longer content to simply have students write about what they are thinking, college professors encourage their students to write about *why* they are thinking what they're thinking. Most college-level writing centers on a thesis, a focusing statement about what students are thinking, followed by evidence that supports their claim and defends it against challengers. Whew. Tough stuff. But not for children who have been writing their minds for so long that they are well prepared to rise to the occasion.

The Link to Technology

With over 90 percent of American children using computers on a daily basis, parents and children alike are understandably excited by all that technology has to offer. And in this technologically advanced millennium, there is no question that the computer has become a quintessential tool for communication. As schools and homes dedicate more resources, both time and money, to technology, writing by hand is falling by the wayside. But the question remains, does modern technology make writing by hand a thing of the past?

Neglecting old-school writing education in favor of its high-tech counterpart is a serious mistake with far-reaching consequences. For young children, a significant developmental opportunity will be missed if a computer is their primary tool for writing. Complex neurological processes occur as our brains guide the movement of our fingers across the page. The process of writing by hand strengthens mind and body connections that underlie attention, coordination, and learning. The movements inherent to writing exercise the brain in ways that a keyboard cannot.

Additionally, children don't even begin to develop effective keyboarding skills until around the third grade. Up until then, children's typing abilities are not efficient enough to keep up with the flow of their ideas. Obviously, waiting until the third grade to learn to write would be another missed opportunity.

A final reason why neglecting writing instruction is detrimental may be the one most compelling to techno-enthusiasts. Computer-savvy individuals are well aware that technology is constantly evolving. Who knows what computing of the future will be like? Already, pen-based computing—in which a pen-like stylus, with the aid of advanced handwriting recognition software, interfaces with a computer—is finding its way into the hands of students and teachers, as well as businesses and industries, across the country. As it turns out, writing may be the new keyboarding.

The Link to Career Success

In the workplace, writing skills are considered a commodity. Written communication is still the most efficient way to reach the greatest number of people. Employers are looking to hire candidates who can compose effective memos, letters, proposals, newsletters, and reports. Strong writing skills are therefore vital to business and professional success.

Between employee and employer, good writing skills communicate clear and purposeful thinking. Businesses in most industries screen job applicants for writing skills, and often don't hire candidates without them. Although it's way too early for kids to start worrying about who will sign their first paycheck, it's never too early to get down to business when it comes to writing. Just think about how children's thank-you notes to Grandma and family newsletters are great practice for their future business correspondence and corporate reports.

The bottom line? Little kids with big aspirations can practically write their own résumé for success by honing their writing skills right from the start.

The Write Way

In order to help guide your children in the "write" direction, it helps to know exactly where you're going. Use this book to build your own foundation, as the parent of a young writer. The first part opens by reflecting on the importance of writing, developmentally speaking. It goes on to highlight the developmental stages related to writing readiness, the best ways to help children build their foundational skills, ideas for equipping children for writing success, and creative ways to encourage and inspire young writers at home. Read through this first part, incorporating whatever information and advice applies to your children (taking into consideration the developmental stages they are at right now) and your particular daily routine. These chapters will provide you with the bare essentials—all the advice and information you need to get your children ready to write.

The second part features fifty-two classic writing activities. Slip one of these projects into your children's writing repertoire when and where it seems to fit, adapting it to their developmental level with the help of the suggested variations. Before long you will find that they will have gained the skills they need to accomplish any writing task that comes their way, and the satisfaction that accompanies the ability to call oneself a writer.

I hope you will find there are a few different ways to use this book. If you are picking it up as the parent of a scribbler, you can use it as a road map to help you guide your child along the path to writing. If your child is already starting to write letters and words, you will find it to be a handy resource to refer to as you support your child's newfound skills. If you are the parent of a reluctant writer, the information in this book is exactly what you need to retrace your child's steps, so to speak. Older children, revisiting their learn-to-write days as they make the transition to cursive, will benefit from reviewing the book's advice and activities as they practice writing in a new style. And if you have multiple children of different ages, you will find that the activity variations in this book are ideal for when your kids are all sitting around the kitchen table—writing thank-you notes, shopping lists, pen-pal letters, or make-believe stories—and you want to figure out how to modify the activity to meet all your kids' needs, no matter their different ages and stages. My hope is that this is a book that will stay on your bookshelf a long time, growing with you and your children—your handbook for helping your family's story unfold.

So now, let's get started. Your mission from here on out is to nurture your young writer until they know this to be true: if you think it, you can write it.

On the Write Track

The Path to Writing Readiness

AT SOME POINT or another most parents have wondered why our precious children were given to us without so much as a handbook to guide us. Luckily, they do come equipped with a roadmap. It's called child development.

As our children's first teachers, we parents need to be as knowledgeable as we can be about child development. Although there is certainly room for individual variation, child development features some general patterns of skill acquisition. Foundational skills are mastered first, and subsequent stages of development are built upon these previously acquired skills. Each developmental stage is characterized by certain major milestones. Being aware of these reference points helps us to plot our course on the road to raising young writers.

The important landmarks children will encounter on the road to writing include scribbling, spelling words, writing stories, and learning the rules of writing.

Scribbles are children's first steps toward writing. As toddling becomes walking and babbling becomes talking, so do scribbles become symbols.

After scribbling, the next steps for young writers include learning to form letters, putting letters together to spell familiar words, and then stringing words together to make sentences and tell stories. Finally, they are ready to learn some of the conventions of writing, such as proper spelling, orienting words on a line, capitalization, punctuation, grammar, and story structure.

To help us identify where our kids are at, and to choose the most appropriate writing activities, I use these landmarks to describe four broad categories of young writers: Scribblers, Spellers, Storytellers, and Scholars.

Scribblers

Scribbling is essentially Writing Readiness 101 for little kids. While creating each messy masterpiece, young children are actually developing and refining the foundational skills that support writing success.

Although it may look random, much is going on during scribbling. As they scribble, children are mastering the motoric challenges of holding and controlling a writing tool. They are experiencing the cause and effect between their movement and their marks, and they are beginning to coordinate their eyes with their hands. They are learning to regulate the speed, force, and direction of their strokes. And they are starting to connect strokes to make shapes, pictures, and symbols that they can use to tell a simple story.

There are even distinct stages that emerge within the scribbling stage. What makes one scribble different from another, you ask? The emergence of recognizable strokes, for example, is one way to quantify scribbling progress. Usually vertical scribbles emerge first, then horizontal, and then circular scribbles.

You can also look for open versus closed strokes. Open strokes are the strokes that go on forever, or back and forth, without a distinct beginning or end (you know those circles that become endless spirals?). Closed strokes have a beginning and an end. They are the starting point for making the shapes that will later turn into drawings and the symbols that will become the letters of the alphabet.

Spellers

Spellers are hard at work learning, practicing, and mastering letter formation. What an important stage! I can't stress enough how critical it is for children to learn the most efficient way to make each letter during this stage. Otherwise they tend to reinvent the wheel each time they make a letter, drawing it instead of writing it automatically. This almost always leads to bad habits that are tough to break later on.

But, fear not! With a little know-how (see the next chapter, "All the Write Moves"), it's as easy as can be to show emerging writers the best way to form each letter. And rest assured, the same techniques are also useful for helping children relearn letter formation if they have already begun making any letters incorrectly.

After Spellers learn to write letters, they start to string them together to form their first written words. What an accomplishment! Cherish and celebrate these first words, awkward invented spellings and all. It is very exciting for children in this stage when they start to put the pieces of the writing puzzle together for the first time. Share in the enthusiasm; this is where a love of writing is born.

Storytellers

If Spellers are excited by first words, Storytellers are simply ecstatic over their first stories. What could be better? This is the stage where all the hard work really begins to pay off. Finally, their skills are starting to catch up to their ideas. They have now mastered the mechanics of writing well enough to be able to "talk on the page." Storytellers are beginning to think like real writers: "What do I want to say?" and "How can I say it?" They get the first taste of the power of writing to tell a tale, transport a reader, create a new world, express emotion, craft a character. Once children begin to write stories, there's no going back. They're hooked.

Scholars

Scholars are writers who have also become readers. As such, they are highly motivated to make their writing resemble the kind of writing they are used to reading. Enter the rules of writing: size and spacing of letters, orientation on a line, capitalization, punctuation, spelling, grammar, sentence structure. Bring them on. Young Scholars are ready to learn the right ways to write.

And they are ready to write *a lot*, in little and big ways, all day long. So prepare yourself (and stock up on paper) because once kids crack the writing code, they tend to be unstoppable.

The Proactive Parent

Now that you know what your *kids* should be doing in each stage, what should *you* be doing to help? Well, here are some of my best tips for supporting young writers in each stage, gleaned from both professional and personal experience.

Supporting Your Scribbler

As you have probably already guessed, I am going to wholeheartedly encourage you to let scribbling happen (almost) whenever and wherever possible (except, of course, on the walls and furniture. Or on younger siblings.). When the opportunity presents itself, you can join in the scribbling too. Sit across from your child and scribble away on your own masterpiece. When you do that, you are teaching by modeling, which means you don't have to instruct. Just have fun yourself, and your child will get the picture. But be careful to stick to scribbling. When we start drawing representational stuff, like flowers, houses, or trains, and writing letters and words, our Scribblers want to follow suit. Since they aren't ready for this yet, they tend to get frustrated and discouraged. They may even lose interest in scribbling and abandon the activity altogether. And what a shame it is when that happens, because they really were having so much fun (*and* working on their foundational skills at the same time). So resist the temptation to rush your Scribbler on to the next stage prematurely. Instead, enjoy letting your inner child bask in the glory of scribbling together with your youngster with reckless abandon.

Remember, also, that a variety of enticing (admittedly, occasionally messy) mediums and methods appeal to young Scribblers. Let them scribble in sand, shaving cream, and finger paint, with sidewalk chalk and tub crayons, while lying on the floor propped up on their elbows or standing at an easel. Hey, with an assiduous Scribbler, anything goes.

Now lest you puzzle over why I don't think it's important to introduce Scribblers to letters, let me assure you that I do. Just not when they're scribbling. Scribblers can work on all the foundational skills that support writing, but they need to work on each component on its own. So certainly expose your Scribbler to alphabet manipulatives, toys, and puzzles, and point out print in books. Just don't expect them to write the letters that they recognize just yet; their scribbles are telling you they need a little more skill-building time before they're ready to write.

Supporting Your Speller

When scribbles begin to morph into lines, shapes, and drawings, you know you will soon have a Speller on your hands. What does your Speller need from you most? During this stage, consider yourself to be a consultant. Offer your expertise on the subject of letter formation or spelling when asked. (Be prepared to be bombarded with countless "How do you make a . . .?" and "How do you spell . . . ?" queries.) And when *you* feel the need for a consultation of your own (to answer your countless "Am I doing this right?" type of questions), refer to the next chapter, which could be alternately titled "Survival Guide for Parents of Spellers."

Supporting Your Storyteller

Every story needs a reader. So, naturally, every Storyteller longs for a captive audience. And who better than an adoring parent to pore over every turn of a phrase, each new tale, or the big magnum opus?

Storytellers are learning to use writing to communicate their ideas. They need parents who are receptive to their stories, no matter whether they are silly or sensible. Try not to critique. Instead, laugh at the funny parts, cry at the sad parts (sniffle, sniffle), and gasp at the surprising parts. There may be plenty of those things that make you go, "Hmmm," but that's all part of the fun. Read on.

Supporting Your Scholar

Scholars can be compared to young athletes, learning the rules of the game. And in this scenario, you should regard yourself as the coach. Help get them psyched for practicing those spelling words or looking up a new word in the dictionary. Gear them up with some cool writing equipment. Help them come up with a game plan for writing that essay or book report (introduction, body, conclusion, hike!). If writing becomes frustrating at any point, call a time out, give a pep talk, talk about strategy, and help them regroup. When it comes time for young Scholars to tackle the transition to cursive writing, go back to basic training (revisiting some of the learn-to-write advice in the next chapter, this time from a script perspective) and help them drill their new writing moves. Keep a watchful eye from the sidelines, and celebrate their writing-related victories with them.

Ready or Not?

So how do you know when your child is ready to move from scribbling to actual writing? Good question. Writing readiness is an important determining factor when it comes to steering kids toward writing success. If a child is still working to master foundational skills, stay there until they're ready to move on. And keep in mind the three most important areas where children need to "get it," before they get down to the business of learning to write.

Get a Clue

A clue about hand preference, that is. In order to be ready to write, children need a strong inclination toward a more skillful, or dominant, hand. This is the hand that is best at executing precise movements. It becomes the go-to hand for any task requiring coordination and control.

If you are unsure as to whether your child has a preferred hand, observe your child eating. Without any prompting on your part, just check out which hand he or she uses to pick up food, both with and without an eating utensil. If your child favors one hand when feeding himself or herself, chances are your child has developed a preference.

Next, watch which hand your child is inclined to use when coloring. If your child sticks with the same hand that he or she chooses to eat with, that's good news. If your child switches back and forth between hands when coloring, he or she may not yet have a clear picture of who's the boss.

Activities such as throwing and catching a ball or cutting with scissors are not ideal for assessing handedness in young children. Kids occasionally approach these tasks with their nondominant hand, which is typically the more powerful hand, at first, switching to their dominant hand, which is more skillful, later on, when the tasks demand better aim or more precise control.

If children seem unclear as to which hand to choose, it is important that we don't do the choosing for them. What we can do, however, is give them plenty of opportunities to engage in bilateral activities that require them to figure out which hand is better at what tasks. Tasks such as mixing batter with one hand (while holding the mixing bowl with the other), spreading butter with a butter knife (while holding the bread steady), or pouring water from a small pitcher (while stabilizing the cup) give children a chance to decide how each hand functions best.

Get a Grip

Some grasps work (and some really, really don't). The rule of thumb is: don't write until it's right!

When I look at how children hold their pencils, I see grasps that fall into three basic categories: immature, efficient, and inefficient.

The grasp that very young children use the first time they pick up a writing tool is usually a *power grasp*. They grab a crayon in a fisted hand, with thumb up and the rest of their fingers wrapped tightly around the shaft of the crayon. All the little muscles in their hands work together to squeeze the crayon in place so that it doesn't move. To make marks, they move their entire arm as a unit, dragging the immobilized crayon back and forth across the page. (Often their other arm, legs, hips, and even their tongue move in unison, going along for the ride.) This difficulty dissociating movements of the hand from movements of the rest of the body is exhausting. No wonder their attention span for this exciting new work is fleeting, at best.

In an attempt to gain more control, most young children soon transition to a *pronated grasp*. With this grasp, all five fingers are still wrapped around the crayon, but now the thumb and fingertips are pointed down toward the paper. Like the power grasp, everything is locked tightly into place. Again, the whole arm has to move in its entirety in order to get the job done.

As they grow more comfortable holding a writing tool, children may experiment with other transitional grasps, such as a *static quadrupod* (four-fingered) grasp or a *static tripod* (three-fingered) grasp. These grasps are referred to as "static" because the fingers still hold very tightly, often high on the shaft of the writing tool, and the whole hand continues to move as one stiff unit.

As children's skills develop and mature, they are better able to isolate out small movements of their hands while stabilizing their wrist, forearm, and upper arm at the shoulder. They are also able to move one side of the hand separately from the other, giving each side of the hand its own function. The thumb side of the hand becomes the skill side, with the first three fingers holding the writing tool like a tripod. The pinky side of the hand becomes the power side, with the fourth and fifth fingers curling into the palm. This side stabilizes the hand on the writing surface, allowing the skill side to move freely.

When children are able to achieve this grasp, which is characterized by smaller, more refined movements by the skill side of the hand, we call it a *dynamic tripod grasp*. This is considered a very efficient grasp because it accomplishes the most controlled movement with the least amount of effort. The dynamic tripod grasp is definitely one to grow on. (See "Anatomy of an Efficient Grasp" on page 202.)

There are a couple of variations on the dynamic tripod grasp that, while less common, are also considered to be efficient grasps. One is the *lateral tripod grasp*, in which the shaft of the pencil is held with the side of the thumb (kind of like how you would hold a key to turn it) rather than with the thumb and index finger being tip to tip. The other is known as an *adaptive tripod grasp*, in which the pencil is stabilized between the index and middle fingers.

What do these efficient grasps have in common? All of them feature some degree of what is referred to as an open web space. That means the triangular-shaped space between the thumb and the index finger (which resembles the "webbing" on a duck's feet) forms a circle when a child holds a pencil. That open space is what gives the fingers on the skill side of the hand the freedom to make their tiny little movements independent of the rest of the hand and arm.

Some children who are attempting to hold a pencil with a tripod grasp collapse that open web space. In order compensate for a lack of control, strength, or stability, they clutch the pencil too tightly, compromising the quality of their grasp. Examples of these inefficient grasps include the *thumb-wrap grasp* (the thumb wraps tightly around both the pencil and the index finger), the *thumb-tuck grasp* (the thumb wraps around the pencil and tucks under the index finger), and the *interdigital brace* (the thumb and second or third fingers wrap tightly around the pencil). What all of these inefficient grasps have in common is a tightly closed web space. This necessitates large movements of the arm and inhibits small, refined movements of the fingers.

Armed with this basic grasp guide, you now have one very important piece of the writing readiness puzzle on your side. Is your child using an efficient grasp when drawing or coloring? If the answer is "Yes," that's one strong indicator in favor of your child being ready to write.

If, however, your child is still using an immature grasp, you have a clear indicator that more writing readiness experiences, including plenty of hand-strengthening activities, are needed.

If your child is using an inefficient grasp, it may be a result of taking on too much too soon. It's best to intervene before these grasps become a fixed habit. Once writing demands increase and children are expected to write more, an inefficient grasp can take its toll. This kind of grasp can make writing slower, more effortful, and at times even painful. It is stressful to the joints of the hands to clench a tool so tightly, often contributing to tired and achy hands. Not to mention unhappy young writers! If you have concerns about your child using an inefficient grasp, discuss it with an occupational therapist (ask your pediatrician or school district for a referral) to determine the best course of action.

> ### DIY: Pencil Picture
>
> As a reminder to children to use a proper pencil position, consider taking a photograph of their hand holding a pencil using an efficient grasp. Place the picture in their writing area to inspire them to use the "just write" grasp each time they pick up a pencil. They can also refer to the drawing on page 202 of the "Anatomy of an Efficient Grasp."

Get in Shape

Children are ready to write when they have mastered the ability to make certain simple shapes. And not before. If your child is still shaky when drawing shapes, it's a clear sign to have them do more drawing before you introduce writing. You see, they are still working on developing what we call visual-motor control, more commonly called eye-hand coordination. And in this case, a picture really is worth a thousand words.

Emerging writers are able to confidently create vertical and horizontal lines, crisscrossed lines, circles, squares, triangles, and diagonal lines. When you see these shapes emerging clearly in your child's drawings, you are getting a strong sense of their readiness to write.

For children whose pencil is not yet cooperating in terms of control, present some fun visual-motor activities for practice. Mazes, dot-to-dot pictures, and coloring activities help children coordinate their eyes with their hand movements; they help kids practice taking aim with their pencils until their visual-motor skills are right on target.

READY OR NOT CHECKLIST

Refer to this checklist to determine whether your child is ready for writing. Your child:

- ☐ Demonstrates a definite hand preference when eating
- ☐ Uses a preferred hand when coloring
- ☐ Is able to use his or her non-preferred hand as a stabilizer during two-handed activities, such as mixing in a bowl or pouring into a cup
- ☐ Holds a crayon, marker, or pencil close to the tip, with the first three (or four) fingers pointed toward the paper when scribbling, coloring, or drawing
- ☐ Is able to draw simple lines and shapes
- ☐ Is beginning to draw people and objects
- ☐ Is starting to make marks that look like symbols
- ☐ Is able to complete simple mazes or dot-to-dot pictures
- ☐ Is beginning to show an interest in staying inside the lines when coloring

So now that you have a better understanding of the landmarks to look for on the road to writing, of your own role in helping to guide your young writers along their course, and of the signs that will signal when your child is ready to write, we move ahead. Preparing your child to progress from scribbling to spelling is the next stop. I can assure you there will be fun, new discoveries and accomplishments up ahead, so enjoy the ride!

All the Write Moves

Preparing Your Child to Write

ARE YOU AS excited as I am to set up your kids for writing success? If you are reading this book, the answer is probably yes. Well, I have good news; since you're looking for information, you're already ahead of the game. Preparing children to write isn't very hard at all, but it does require a little bit of know-how. Luckily, this chapter can be your everything-you-ever-needed-to-know guide to helping your child progress from Scribbler to Speller, and beyond.

So if it's supposed to be simple, what's there to know? Basically, it's a matter of pointing our kids in the right direction. When it comes to teaching the skills that support writing, my motto is this: teach them right, right from the start. Learning the best strategies, right from the get-go, prevents children from getting into bad habits or expending more effort than necessary on writing tasks (and, as a result, thinking that writing is hard or that they don't like it). Steering them onto the right path, however, makes learning to write so natural that children will think they were born to write.

Write Now

As parents, we want the best for our children in many different ways. Why not give them the best possible start on their journey as writers? Starting them off right can mean the difference between struggle and success. It can also be the deciding factor between children who work hard at writing and children who write so effortlessly that their ideas all but leap onto the page. Happily, for children who embrace writing, a lifetime love of learning is literally right at their fingertips.

Here are the top ten things you can do to get your kids ready to write.

1. You Can Teach a Child the Best Way to Hold a Pencil (Yes, You!)

My son showed an interest in pencils early on. He liked to feed them into the sharpener, wear one behind his ear like a carpenter, and mark his wood blocks before "cutting" them with his pretend saw. But when it came time to write with a pencil, his enthusiasm was tested. Why? Because holding a pencil is an acquired skill, one that requires practice.

Most children learn to use a pencil between the ages of three and a half and five. More important than age, however, are signs of readiness. Look for a consistent hand preference, interest in coloring and drawing with crayons, coordinated use of eating utensils, and ability to handle clothing fasteners. Mastery of these tasks means that your child's little fingers have pencil-holding potential.

When teaching your child to get a grip, demonstrate these important pencil pointers:

* *Pinch* the pencil (low on the shaft, just above the zigzag part) between the pad of the thumb and the tip of the index finger. The space between the two fingers should form a wide-open circle. Check to see that your child is using a light touch (no white knuckles!).
* *Tuck* the third finger behind, so the pencil leans on the side of the first joint.
* *Squeeze* the fourth and fifth fingers into the palm, and rest this side of the hand on the writing surface.

At first, it's best to have children practice this new grasp by doing things other than writing. For example, tracing stencils and drawing activities sharpen pencil skills without the added challenge of forming letters.

Children who can't get their fingers in the right position may need more time with tools that encourage a three-fingered grasp. The best pencil prep is having your child use tiny broken crayons or pieces of chalk to color or scribble. Other activities that strengthen the pencil-holding muscles are: stringing beads, spraying a spray bottle, manipulating play dough, and cutting with scissors.

What's the point of all this practice? An efficient pencil grasp lays the groundwork for fluid writing. And holding a pencil right, right from the start, prevents a child from getting into bad habits that may interfere with writing success down the road. Let's just say, it's a big step in the "write" direction.

> ## DIY: Give Me a Break Crayons
>
> If your child has a shaky grasp on pencils, it may be time for a little break. Time for a little crayon breaking, that is.
>
> Scribbling, coloring, drawing, or writing with crayons broken into small pieces encourages a three-fingered grasp. Simply peel and break some crayons into pieces to give the little muscles involved in holding a pencil a fun (and colorful) workout. (Caution: tiny tools can be a choking hazard, so exercise care with the under-three crowd.)

2. Tweak the Rules for Lefties

I am often asked if there are any special considerations for left-handed writers when it comes to holding a pencil. The answer is a resounding "Yes!"

Because the English language is written left to right, writing with the left hand is not simply the reverse of writing with the right one. When it comes to writing, lefties encounter a couple of unique challenges. First of all, their hands cover up the words as they write, making it difficult for them to see their own work. And second, they have a tendency to smudge their writing with their hands as they move across the page.

To help left-handed children overcome these challenges, teach them the three important rules to improve their view (and prevent smudging):

* *Pinch it higher:* Pinch the pencil slightly farther up on the shaft (about one to one and a half inches from the tip).
* *Position the paper:* Shift the paper to the left of center in front of them and tilt it slightly toward the right.

* *Point it:* Hold the pencil so that the eraser points toward their left shoulder; this helps to keep their hand below the writing line.

These simple writing rules will make a big difference for lefties, helping them write with greater comfort and ease. And if it seems a little frustrating at first, assure your young writers that they are in good company: many famous authors (including Hans Christian Andersen, Lewis Carroll, and Mark Twain), artists (including Michelangelo, Leonardo da Vinci, and Picasso), movers and shakers (including Albert Einstein, Benjamin Franklin, and Helen Keller), and eight U.S. presidents were highly successful southpaws.

3. Every Writer Needs a Helping Hand, Literally

While one hand gets a grip on the pencil, what's the other hand doing? Certainly not twiddling its thumb. The role of the nondominant hand is to stabilize the paper during writing tasks. The importance of this seemingly simple contribution cannot be overemphasized. Without a helper hand, the paper slips and slides, making the process of writing unmanageable and the product unreadable.

You can help your children get accustomed to using a lead-assist pattern with their hands by cueing them to use their "boss" hand and "helper" hand during everyday activities. For example, you can remind your children to stabilize their bowls with their helper hand when eating cereal or mixing cake batter. Or remind them to hold the bottom of their sweatshirt with a helper hand while their boss hand pulls up the zipper. The more aware children are of their helper hands, the more likely they will use them to get ready (and steady) to write.

DIY: Handy Helper

If your children need frequent reminders to use their nondominant hand, this trick may help. First, have them trace their non-dominant hand on a piece of colored paper. Then, have them cut out the hand shape. Not only are tracing and cutting two great activities that reinforce the use of the helper hand, but the resulting cutout can be taped to the top corner of a piece of paper as a visual cue reminding children to steady the page as they write.

4. Strong Writing Starts with Strong Hands

Mastering the use of their hands is one of our children's greatest and most rewarding accomplishments. Children use their hands to interact with the world. They use them to play with toys, feed themselves, show affection, get dressed, cut with scissors, paint a picture, and scribble their thoughts. Children's hands help them perform all the meaningful occupations of childhood. For this reason, time spent building fine motor skills is, without a doubt, time well spent.

Moreover, where writing is concerned, strong hand skills are the very key to success. Creating a hands-on home is not only the first step toward raising competent kids, it's also the best way to prepare little hands for the big job of writing.

There are countless opportunities for kids to be hands-on throughout their day. From making their own meals to making mud pies, children who are encouraged to experiment and explore gain the upper hand, so to speak. They become proficient in the small, refined movements needed to accomplish tasks with skill and precision. And they learn that they can do it themselves, figure it out, make it work, and get it done. Essential for all children, these experiences are especially important for young children who are getting ready to write.

Some of my favorite fine-motor activities include the following:

> making and playing with homemade play dough
> cutting coupons or junk mail with scissors

FYI: Squeeze Please

Our favorite, no-fail play dough recipe:

2 cups water

1 cup salt

2 tablespoons cream of tartar

2 tablespoons vegetable oil

food coloring

2 cups flour

Heat all ingredients except the flour in a saucepan until warm. Remove the pan from the heat and stir in the flour. Scoop the dough out of the pan and onto a cookie sheet. Let it cool for a few minutes, and then knead it well until all the color is evenly distributed and the dough is a smooth texture. Store the dough in an airtight container for up to six months.

---

picking up small objects with kitchen tongs
using small stampers with a stamp pad
stringing beads
watering plants or a garden with a spray bottle
clipping clothespins on a line

Then, of course, there are the everyday activities that provide great fine-motor challenges. Make sure you help your children learn to do the following things independently, and they will reap the benefits on a daily basis:

buttoning, zippering, and snapping clothes
fastening shoes
opening containers
opening and closing resealable plastic bags
using eating utensils
helping with meal preparations
wiping a table with a sponge

The bottom line is, where kids are concerned, a hands-on home is a happy home. Children who have abundant opportunities to develop their fine-motor skills are well prepared for writing, and for life. Wherever they go, they'll take with them the confidence that comes from experience. And however they make their mark, they'll do it with broad strokes and self-assurance.

5. Cutting Isn't Just a Frill

Everyone knows that young children should learn to cut. We all realize that cutting is necessary for many classroom tasks and some daily activities. Yet there is another reason why cutting is so important that may surprise you. Did you know that when done correctly, cutting can actually improve your child's handwriting?

When children are taught to cut the "write" way, every snip helps to strengthen the small intrinsic muscles of their hands. These are the same muscles that control that all-important tripod grasp, the most efficient pencil grasp for writing.

The "write" grasp of the scissors is the one that exercises the small muscles that are needed to achieve a mature tripod grasp. Children should be taught to hold the scissor with the thumb and *middle* finger in the loops. The index finger should be placed on the *outside* of the handle to provide strength and to direct the cutting activity. Fingers four and five should be curled into the palm for stability. The scissors should be held loosely against the hand, resting on the joints of the fingers closest to the fingertips. The scissors should always be held in a "thumbs up!" position and pointed away from the child at all times.

How do you know if your child is ready for scissors? Cutting requires hand strength, eye-hand coordination, and finger dexterity. If your children are able to manipulate play dough effectively, activate squirt toys or spray bottles, string beads on a lace, and rip paper into small pieces with ease, then they have some important prerequisite skills. But the most important prerequisite skill, by far, is your child's establishment of a hand preference. Wait to introduce scissors to your child until you see your child favoring one hand over the other during tasks such as eating, playing, or coloring.

Cutting, at least initially, is a one-to-one activity, and parents make the best teachers. Remember, even though scissors are available at your child's preschool, teachers have many pairs of little hands to watch at the same time. Give your little snippers individual attention at first, and you will find them sharpening their scissor skills in no time.

Important Safety Note: Cutting requires hands-on adult supervision at all times. When not in use, scissors should be kept securely out of the reach of children. Children should also be taught the proper way to hold scissors when carrying them and how to safely hand them to another person. And don't forget to teach that classic old-school rule: "No running with scissors!"

6. Big Muscles Support Little Muscles

Writing is not purely a paper-and-pencil activity. Nor is it strictly a cerebral pursuit. Writing is a whole-body activity, like playing sports, learning to dance, or riding a bicycle. It requires coordination, strength, and stamina. When children are writing, every muscle is at work, either stabilizing the body or controlling the skilled movements of the hand.

Although it may seem like a stretch, running and jumping, hopping and skipping, climbing and crawling, throwing and catching actually prepare children for writing. These activities are definitely part of the core curriculum for young writers. They build and reinforce the foundational skills that support writing-skill development. And skills built on a strong foundation are built to last.

It is important to incorporate some big-muscle time into every day, which we probably do instinctively anyway due to our awareness of the many benefits of exercise. We have already learned through experience that regular physical activities keep our kids healthier, calmer, happier, and in better shape.

Well, now you can add another item to your list of reasons why a daily "workout" just makes good sense: writing readiness. Strong bodies produce confident strokes, coordinated children control their pencils better, and kids with physical stamina have more endurance for seated tasks that require sustained attention.

Despite this, some schools are cutting down on physical education or cutting out recess altogether. Don't let this happen to your kids! Advocate for their gross-motor needs as passionately as you would for their academic needs. The two go hand in hand. And try to avoid restricting physical activities when your children haven't finished their work. This penalty is counterproductive, both at home and in school. The fact of the matter is children who are struggling to get their work done probably need to jump-start their minds and bodies with some movement. A little big-muscle play may be all they need to get their writing muscles in gear.

In addition to the backyard, the playground, and the schoolyard, my all-time favorite big-muscle activities for children include the following:

> wheelbarrow walking (hold your children's feet as they walk on their hands)
> walking on a balance beam (or a low curb)
> hanging from monkey bars (or a chin-up bar)
> crawling (through tunnels, around the house, over pillows, and so on)
> playing catch
> playing balloon volleyball
> jumping on a mini trampoline

Big-muscle activities are just about the most fun you can have as a kid. Aren't we lucky that they make a big impact developmentally too? So when in doubt, let kids go out and play.

7. Read the Writing on the Wall

The writing on the wall is clear: going vertical is one of the best ways to pump up the writing muscles.

I'm referring of course to vertical surfaces.

Any activity that is done on a vertical surface strengthens the shoulder muscles by encouraging them to work against gravity. Each time children reach up and out, they are developing the stability that promotes mobility. Simple activities done at arm's reach support writing development by helping children become stable and able.

Encourage your children to try the following on-the-wall activities whenever possible:

> painting or drawing at an easel
> drawing on a chalkboard
> playing with magnets on a refrigerator or magnet board
> drawing on a dry-erase board
> playing with shapes and figures on a felt board
> drawing or putting stickers on a large piece of paper taped to a wall
> drawing on bathtub walls with tub crayons
> "washing" windows or shower doors with water
> "painting" outdoor walls or fences with a large paintbrush and water
> using sidewalk chalk on outdoor walls

Any way you look at it, elevating the writing surface is a surefire way to take children's writing readiness to the next level.

8. Sit for Success

Postural control is the backbone of good writing skills. Writing without postural control is like writing on a moving bus: nearly impossible and barely legible.

Postural control is the key to our ability to achieve and maintain a steady stance. Our trunk provides a base of support for moving our extremities. When our posture is even slightly unstable, our limbs pitch in to help hold us up, compromising their ability to complete the task at hand. When we have adequate control of our posture, we free up our arms (and hands) to function. Simply stated, stability is at the core of mobility.

When it comes time to write, the secret to postural control lies in how children sit at a desk. Assuming their desks and chairs are the proper height (this is important; see the chapter on "The Write Stuff"), there are four factors that will promote good posture:

* Their feet should be flat on the floor in front of them.
* Their hips should be slid all the way to the back of the chair.
* Their paper should be positioned properly.
* Their helper hand should be stabilizing the paper.

Then (and only then) are they ready to begin.

Knowing this, I came up with a quickie four-step routine that I do with kids every time they sit down. The ritual of it becomes habit before long, until, eventually, the optimal posture becomes second nature.

Run through the steps as soon as your kids take a seat; it only takes a few seconds, at most. When your kids get the hang of it, they'll start doing it on their own. The steps are:

1. *Stomp:* Show your children how to stomp their feet on the floor when they sit down. The force of the stomping sends a powerful message to their brain that reinforces the idea that feet should be planted firmly on the floor.
2. *Slide:* Show your kids how to slide their hips back until they bump the back of their chair. This ensures an upright posture and prevents kids from rounding their backs or slouching in their chair.
3. *Slant:* When they're seated, have your kids slant their paper slightly (approximately twenty degrees to the left for righties; up to twenty degrees to the right and shifted slightly to the left of center for lefties).
4. *Slap:* Finally, have your kids slap down their helper hand at the top corner of their paper to reinforce the idea that they have to stabilize their paper. Again, we slap because (like stomping)

it's intense enough to send a loud-and-clear message to the brain: "Do this!"

9. Teaching Children the Right Way to Write Letters Makes a Huge Difference, Both Now and Later On (Huge, Trust Me)

If you're planning on going somewhere new, there are a couple of ways you could go about it. You could map out your trip beforehand, finding the most direct route between point A and point B. Or you can meander toward your destination, making decisions on a whim. You could choose to turn or go straight depending on what looks interesting, or where you think you are in relation to your destination. You could make up your route as you go, correcting yourself if you go in the wrong direction, starting over again if you get totally lost. Will you get where you're going? Possibly. Eventually. But at what cost? Maybe you wasted time, got frustrated, or felt confused. Or maybe you gave up and never got there at all.

Comparatively, the first approach is definitely the most efficient one. It has another big advantage as well: it is easily reproducible. The next time you are headed for the same place, you can follow the same map. And the next time. And the time after that. After several successful attempts, you probably won't even need the map anymore. You'll know the way by heart.

At the beginning, it may have taken a few extra minutes to figure out the best path. But boy, was that time well spent in the long run. Not only was taking the most efficient route successful, it facilitated learning as well.

The same holds true for learning to write the letters of the alphabet, of course. Plotting each letter's path, right from the start, sets kids up for success. With just a bit of practice they will internalize the way and make it their own. Their writing will become efficient and automatic, as if someone hit the cruise control button.

Children who teach themselves to write, however, are often at a disadvantage. They meander along when it comes to letter formation. When you watch them write, you get the sense that they're reinventing the wheel with every letter they attempt. They seem to draw each letter, as opposed to writing it, tinkering with it until it looks just right. Easily frustrated (and with a tendency to accumulate a collection of crumpled papers), they focus too much attention on the *how* of writing at the expense of *what* they are writing. They certainly may get where they're going, but, by the time they arrive, they're so exhausted, they're not sure they ever want to go back.

Luckily, this is *easily* preventable with a little help. And I actually mean a little. This isn't tough stuff we're talking about here. (If it was, would someone have coined the term, "As easy as learning your ABCs"?) Sure, it's a little effort up front. But like teaching your children to tie their own shoelaces, pedal a two-wheeler, or look both ways before crossing the street, it's a sound investment with big rewards. The payoff is kids who are off and running on their own. So very worth it.

DIY: Alphabet Chart

Copy the alphabet chart on page 203 from the templates section, or use it as a guide to make your own chart using markers and large paper or poster board, and post it by your child's writing space. Looking at each letter with its arrow guides is the best way for children to realize that every letter has its own road map. By placing this chart in your children's writing area, you are teaching them to follow the best path when writing (and that it's okay to ask for directions).

Here are a few basic alphabet-writing rules to live by:

1. Always start letters at the top, and make all vertical strokes from top to bottom.
2. Make horizontal strokes from left to right (to be efficient, letter strokes should move in the same direction that writing moves across the page, so your hand isn't going back and forth).
3. Make circular strokes (capital *C, G, O,* and *Q* and lowercase *a, c, d, e, g,* and *q*) in a counterclockwise direction.
4. To prevent reversals in the most commonly flip-flopped letters, *b* and *d,* teach these letters using different movements. Lowercase *b* starts with a straight line down and then has a small curve, while lowercase *d* starts with the small curve (as if you were writing a *c*) and then adds a straight line down. Mind your *ps* and *qs* as well: *p* starts with the line down and then the curve; *q* starts with the curve (like a *c*) and then the line down.

10. Multisensory Learning Rocks!

When it's time for your children to learn to write their ABCs, there's no better way to start than by putting the shape of each letter right in the palms of their hands.

It's one thing to sing the ABCs, or to recognize them by sight. Getting a *feel* for the alphabet, on the other hand, is something else entirely. And a feel for the alphabet is exactly what children need in order to learn to write.

This is because the alphabet is not just a set of little picture symbols or a collection of sounds. Each letter is also a movement. (For example, *A* is a big downhill line, hop back to the top, downhill the other way, and a little line across. *B* is a big line straight down, hop back to the top, and make two little curves. And *C* is one great big curved line down. Get the picture?) Each letter has its own unique choreography. If children learn the right moves, their writing will dance across the page gracefully. If they make up the steps as they go along, however, writing becomes a struggle along the lines of dancing with two left feet.

When children manipulate three-dimensional letters (such as alphabet puzzle pieces or magnetic alphabet letters), they get to run their fingers along the lines and curves as they look at each letter and say its sound. The touch system sends information to the brain along with the visual and auditory systems. What a learning experience! Multisensory information makes the brain positively light up from all of the connections it is making. In other words, when children's brains process input along several sensory channels at the same time, everything just makes more sense.

In addition to manipulating letters, children can also get a feel for letters by putting together their component pieces. For example, Handwriting Without Tears (see the resources at the end of the book) has a set of generously sized wood lines and curves that can be used to build all the capital letters.

Once children have gotten in touch with the letters, it's time for them to work on their moves. Their letter moves, of course.

When you first introduce letter movements to children, think big. Gross-motor movements are the easiest for young children to imitate. Children can practice "writing" letters in the air using large, sweeping arm movements. Big movements send big feedback to kids' brains. This also helps them experience success at learning the movements of writing, by isolating out the fine-motor factor. In other words, children can concentrate on the concept of letter formation, without struggling to control their tiny finger muscles at the same time.

Want another great way to get emerging writers to focus on letter formation? Try writing on them. Yeah, I'm serious. Only skip the ink and use your finger instead. Trace letters in the palms of their hands or on their backs. Once they get the picture, so to speak, write little messages on them, such as "I love you" or "You are cute."

When it's time to take it to the next level, combine tactile input with the movements learned to create the ultimate multisensory learning experience. I have found sand to be the perfect medium for providing really powerful feedback for practicing writers. Fill a shallow box or tray with about a

---

DIY: Touchy-Feely Letters

When you combine the sights and sounds of letter shapes with tactile and movement input, information travels along an express train to the brain. Showing a child how to trace over sand letters with their finger capitalizes on the multisensory connection.

MATERIALS
colored index cards (unlined)

glue

sand

box for storing cards (optional)

HOW-TO

1. "Draw" a letter of the alphabet with glue on an index card. If your child is right-handed, place the letter to the right of center on the card; if your child is left-handed, place it to the left of center. (This allows room for children to stabilize the card with their helper hands while tracing.)
2. Sprinkle sand over the glue, covering it thoroughly.
3. Wait two to three minutes, and then shake off excess sand. Let it dry.
4. When the letter is completely dry, show your children how to trace over it (following the right path) with their fingers, while saying the letter sound out loud.

---

half inch of sand, and then show your children how to practice writing their letters.

Which letters should you show kids first? The letters of their name (first letter capital, the rest lowercase) are a great place to start. Then, instead of presenting letters in alphabetical order, try progressing from easiest to hardest. The easiest letters to write are made up of straight lines, then come curves, and finally letters with diagonal lines.

Remember, you can also retrace many of these steps with older children who are beginning the process of learning to write in cursive. (I've included a cursive alphabet chart in the templates section on page 204, for future reference). Newbie cursive writers need to master new letter movements, and they will surely benefit from this approach as well. It definitely beats learning penmanship by writing over and over again in a copybook, like they did in the good old days.

Whether letters are manuscript or cursive, multisensory experiences bring them to life for children. Try them, and you'll see (and feel) what I mean.

Write On

On a final note, I'll quote my son, who told me emphatically, at the wise old age of four: "You know, things don't have to be perfect to be just right." So very true indeed, especially when it comes to learning to write.

In the early stages of writing, it's much more important to help children learn the right process of forming letters, without focusing too heavily on the product. If my writing wishes could all come true, I would much rather see children learning all the right moves rather than achieving perfect penmanship at the expense of efficient, effective methods that will better serve them down the road.

Writing is "just right" when it flows easily from a child's hand without excessive effort. Children's minds should be free to focus on the content of their writing without getting overly bogged down by worrying about mechanics. Good habits learned early are the secret to pointing children in the right direction, writing-wise. And once our young writers are on their way, well, let's just say they can pretty much write their own ticket to anywhere they want to go.

The Write Stuff

Tools, Materials, and Spaces
That Promote Writing

T O TURN AN IDEA into reality, a young writer requires only a few simple tools. Like a carpenter who always looks into his toolbox for a hammer and nails, a child needs only the most basic tools—a pencil and paper—to build a story. Add some crayons to young writers' toolboxes, a handful of colored pencils, maybe a few washable markers, and writers will be geared up for constructing an endless array of bright ideas.

The just-right tools get the job done. Decidedly un-fancy, they seem to pale in comparison to the bells-and-whistles educational toys on the shelves. But don't be fooled. Even though batteries aren't included, that small cardboard box of crayons or forty-nine-cent pack of pencils has a power all its own. The less that an "educational" thing does by itself right out of the box, the more children are required to do for themselves. No-frills writing tools are educational in the truest sense of the word, not to mention empowering, and that is, of course, priceless.

Well-equipped young writers are ready for anything. With a natural sense of wonder, newly acquired skills, and good tools at their disposal, they are all set to rise to the occasion. A parent's role at this stage is easy yet essential. Simply keep a stash of writing tools well-stocked and within reach. And remember, when it comes to useful utensils, you can't beat the basics. Why? Because children have a wealth of amazing stories inside them already. All they need are a few carefully chosen tools to help them get their ideas out and onto the page.

Tools of the Trade

More than mere school supplies, writing tools are required gear for kids at home too. From pencils to markers, crayons to chalk, these simple tools are a young writer's self-expression essentials.

Pencils

Seriously underrated in this age of techno gadgetry, the pencil has been the workhorse of both young and established writers for generations. And although it may not be able to send and receive text messages (yet), it gets points for working underwater *and* in outer space, writing fifty thousand words without having to be charged or plugged in, and having its own built-in delete function. All that for about ten cents a pop. Not bad at all.

Pencils are a wonderfully forgiving medium for young writers. Like a tiny beacon perched on top, that little eraser reassures, "Don't worry! Everyone makes mistakes. No problem!"

Pencils are also available in varieties beyond the familiar No. 2. For example, newbie writers might like a softer lead (such as is found in drafting pencils), which makes a darker mark on paper with less effort.

> ### FYI: Get the Lead Out
>
> Pencil leads are actually lead-free (and always have been). Pencils make marks using graphite, a nontoxic carbon-based substance. Before the discovery of graphite, the ancient Romans used lead to make light marks on parchment, leading them to mistakenly call graphite "black lead" when they found that it made similar yet darker marks.
>
> However, the paint covering pencils can contain trace amounts of lead. Pencils certified by the Pencil Makers Association conform to regulatory standards regarding lead in the paint, so look for the PMA seal when your purchase your pencils. But if you have a pencil biter at home, opt for unpainted pencils, just to be safe.

Shape and size can make pencils more comfortable for developing hands to hold. I prefer smaller pencils for new writers. Golf pencils work well, but they don't have an eraser, which many kids miss. So I usually modify standard pencils by snipping a few inches off the end with pliers before I sharpen them. Triangular-shaped pencils are also worth a try. Some children find them easier to hold because they can put one finger on each of the three sides, making it slightly easier to achieve the sought-after tripod grasp.

For children who crave a little more bling than the basic pencil has to offer, there is a plethora of ways to personalize your pencil. There are pencils with pictures of favorite characters, exciting pencil toppers, pencils with built-in grips, even pencils scented with your child's favorite flavor. There are "green" pencils made from recycled materials such as newspapers and (yes!) car tires. And, of course, mechanical pencils can dispense leads with a mere click (sharpener not required).

Pens

All kids are eager to try their hand at writing with a pen, because that's what they see the grown-ups doing. Pens, however, present some unique challenges for children. They need to be held at a precise angle. Only the perfect amount of pressure will result in a mark. The ink smudges (especially if you are a leftie). If children hold the pen at an awkward angle or use a light touch, even for a moment, their writing disappears. How frustrating! Luckily there are plenty of other, more suitable, options.

Crayons

Crayons are an ideal medium for emerging writers because they provide valuable feedback to little hands learning their craft. When children apply light pressure on a crayon they get a fine, faint mark. Firm pressure produces strong, bold strokes. And since every color imaginable is offered in the iconic box of sixty-four, they inspire a full spectrum of self-expression.

Colorful crayons can be like eye candy to children, so, although it's wonderful to have a full range of colors available, you might not want to offer them all at once. The sheer volume of choices can be overwhelming and may even distract from the task at hand. I tend to present the rainbow of options in a way that is enticing (I like to keep them in a glass jar), and invite kids to choose a few of their favorite colors before they get to work. Then I put the big container aside. That way the choice is all theirs, but they can move on from the decision making and get on with the work of creating.

High-quality beeswax and soy-based crayons are a luxury appreciated by the artistically inclined, but definitely are not essential for writing success. Typical petroleum-based wax crayons are the best choice for prolific young writers; they are a good quality and affordable staple to stock up on.

Another advantage of these crayons is that they are sharpened to a point, which offers better control for more distinct marks. Eventually, as children's writing improves and they are able to write more words at a smaller size, crayons will no longer be the tool of choice for writing. Yet they will continue to be useful indefinitely, for illustrating all the short stories of childhood.

Colored Pencils

Functionally speaking, colored pencils are actually more closely related to crayons than pencils. Like their waxy cousins, colored pencils are good for early letter-writing practice. They vary considerably in quality, however, so it's good to test them out to make sure they make a smooth mark without excessive effort.

There is one important (and apparent) way that colored pencils resemble the graphite variety: their shape. This similarity comes in very handy. You see, every time kids use colored pencils, even if they are using them for activities other than writing, they are reinforcing and refining their pencil grasp. Any creating that incorporates colored pencils therefore supports writing, making them a young writer's best friend.

> ### FYI: Size Wise
>
> If you're shopping for writing supplies for your children, you may realize you're getting some mixed messages. Some items, like primary pencils and chubby crayons, are oversized, supposedly easier for small hands to grasp. Other items, like mini markers and colored pencils, are scaled more in proportion to smaller hands. What's up with that?
>
> For beginning writers, I choose tiny tools for little hands. Oversized utensils can be hard to maneuver, heavy, and difficult to control. Smaller tools encourage the small muscles to do what they're supposed to do, and put little hands in a position of greater control.

Markers

There's a reason they call them "magic" markers. These aptly named tools are so responsive, kids think they're just amazing.

Right out of the box they produce consistently colorful print. No matter whether a young writer is self-assured or tentative, bold streaks of color appear with seemingly little effort. They are the great equalizer of writing tools, always responding to both the big and small movements of little hands with vibrant marks.

The downside of markers is they can be high maintenance. But teach your children to care for their markers (constantly replacing caps is a must), and it will soon become habit. And be sure to pluck dried-up markers out of the bunch as soon as you notice them so they don't dull your kids' brilliant ideas.

Chalk

Oh, chalk. How do I love thee? Let me count the ways. (1) You are so tactile. You help children to really *feel* their movements as they write, which sends so much valuable information to their eager-to-learn brains. (2) You are so easily correctable. A swipe of the finger, sweep of an eraser, or wipe with a cloth is all it takes to fix any slip-ups. (3) You provide a perpetual blank slate for young writers-in-training. Because your marks disappear, children's inhibitions about writing vanish as well.

Not to go overboard, but chalk (white or colored) really is my favorite

---

DIY: Quill Pencils

Whimsical quill pencils will tickle any young writer's fancy. Luckily, they're super easy to whip up.

MATERIALS

colored pencils
colored craft feathers
white glue
embroidery floss

HOW-TO

1. Glue the stem of a colored feather to the top of a colored pencil. Let it dry.
2. Apply more glue to the top of the pencil. Starting at the top and working your way down, wrap embroidery floss around the pencil until you have covered the bottom of the feather.
3. Cut the embroidery floss, and fasten the cut end to the pencil with a final drop of glue.

Write and have fun!

medium for the early stages of learning to write. I have seen so many children learn to write by making and erasing chalk marks over and over until they get it right. I imagine that's where the expression "chalk it up to experience" comes from!

The Resourceful Writer

I've been known to write grocery lists on paper plates. My husband jots lumber orders and important measurements on scraps of wood. We're in good company: Abraham Lincoln did his homework on the back of a shovel, Ernest Hemingway wrote on napkins, and our national anthem was drafted on an envelope. It seems that, no matter what, determined writers can always find a place to document their thoughts.

Children likewise record their ideas wherever they can because they just can't help themselves. Covering a blank canvas with their own one-of-a-kind combination of words is irresistibly exciting for young writers. It is a rite of passage to scribble, scrawl, sign your name, and share your story on as many surfaces as you can. At the end of the day, all those little scraps left behind testify, "I left my mark on the world today."

Henry David Thoreau observed: "The world is but a canvas to our imagination." (Spoken like someone who's never had to clean crayon off the living room walls!) Happily, there are many interesting (and acceptable) canvases upon which young writers can express their creativity. From butcher paper to bathtub walls, sidewalks to sand, almost anything can become a blank slate for a resourceful writer.

Paper: Plain or Lined?

I remember when I first got my learner's permit; my parents took me to a big, empty parking lot to drive for the first time. It was there I was able to get the "feel" of driving. After a while, we ventured onto local streets, choosing the extra-wide streets (hard to come by in the city) to work on my parallel parking skills. Finally, license in hand, I braved a multilane highway (white knuckles and all).

Similar logic applies to choosing paper for little learners. When kids are first starting to write letters and words, big unlined paper works best. At this stage, the most important thing is that they get a feel for letter formation.

Later, when you see that their letters have become consistently smaller in size, indicating greater control, paper with extra-wide guidelines is appropriate. When they become more skillful at writing words and sentences, they are ready to handle ruled paper.

When it comes to lined paper, there are more varieties available than you can imagine. There is paper with two guidelines per line of writing, three guidelines (including a dashed middle line), and four guidelines (featuring an upper and lower line to direct ascenders and descenders). Some papers color code the lines so that children can distinguish between the baseline and the other lines.

Personally, I find the multilined, color-coded papers to be confusing. And if I can't keep track of which line is which, how can I expect a child to figure it out? I opt for standard lined paper, wide-ruled first and college-ruled much later. After all, the lines are just meant to help kids steer their writing in the

DIY: Letterhead

My son often sits at his desk and shuffles things about in a very important way. When I ask him what he's doing, he proudly replies, "Paperwork!"

Kids get the fact that the work we do at our desks is serious business. And they are eager to conduct some busy-ness of their own. Set them up with some personalized letterhead to give their writing a professional flair.

MATERIALS

computer

printer

blank printer paper

HOW-TO

1. Using a basic word-processing program, put your child's name, address, and phone number on the top of a blank document (an added bonus is that it helps them learn this important information).
2. Print out multiple copies.
3. Be sure to save the document on your hard drive so you can restock inventory as needed.

right direction. If they are overly focused on the lines (or overly distracted by them) they are liable to veer off course.

Courtney Casey
33 Big Hill Road
Playville, NY 11358

Dear Jack,

Can you come over to my house to play? Tell your mom to call my mom.

Love,
Courtney

Notebooks

Children who have been read to since their earliest days have a happy reverence for books. That's why it is especially exciting for them to write in one. To actually put their own ideas on those inviting blank pages, inserting their thoughts between those important-looking covers, is impressive. Yes, books make young writers feel bona fide.

Notebooks definitely give little kids that big-kid feeling. They are also great for a more thorough study of an interesting idea. Better than a piece of paper, a notebook can hold a whole series of scribbles, a day-to-day account of the amazing adventures of a favorite superhero stuffed animal, or an in-depth research study of cafeteria mystery meat. It is the perfect place to jot down clues, secrets, notes from a fact-finding mission, lists, dreams, wishes. More personal than a piece of paper, a notebook has covers that can be closed, like a bedroom door, making it more likely that children will put their true feelings on the page.

There are plenty of notebooks to choose from. Hardcover, softcover, and spiral notebooks, as well as three-ring binders filled with notebook paper, all come in both plain and fancy styles. Kids love to embellish the simple ones with stickers, names, and sayings. They also love notebooks with pictures of their favorite characters, sports figures, animals, and whatnot. Whatever helps them to own their books will no doubt encourage them to write as well.

Sticky Notes

Kids are instantly attracted to those sticky little repositionable notes. Dole them out carefully, however; they can go through a whole pack in a matter of minutes. What's the appeal? Let's just say there's a serious wow factor in being able to plaster your ideas all over the place. Sticky notes make it okay to "write" on the walls, the floor, the ceiling (if you can reach), the furniture, your little sister, the dog . . . well, you get the idea. There's endless fun involved in labeling your surroundings, captioning the action, or leaving a trail of thoughts for someone to follow like breadcrumbs. Hand over a pack every now and again, and just see what happens!

Butcher Paper, Kraft Paper, and Newsprint

At my office, a bright boy named T. J. was a mile-a-minute talker full of captivating stories. I was (and still am) convinced that he will someday pen the next great American novel. But whenever he sat in front of a pencil and paper, he got very quiet. No more stories. Reluctant to even pick up the pencil, he resisted writing in a big way.

That was until I brought out the *big* paper. The day I unrolled a giant roll of butcher paper, T. J. wrote up a storm. Words, pictures, arrows, diagrams, you name it. It all came out. At the end of our time together, T. J. rolled up about twelve feet of work with a self-satisfied sigh, tucked it under his arm, and marched proudly down the hall. Apparently his ideas were a little too big for an 8½ x 11 inch page. The small size seemed to stifle him. From that day on he gravitated to the big paper roll and generated writing by the mile.

Since children *think* big, they love having the option to *write* big. Try spreading a big sheet of paper out on the floor or across a table, hanging it on the wall mural-style, or clipping it onto an easel. Stand back and watch what happens. But be prepared—big paper tends to inspire larger-than-life ideas. You may have to move some furniture (or put an extension on the house!).

Butcher paper is available in large rolls at restaurant supply stores, or you can ask your local butcher to sell you some. Brown kraft paper can be found at craft stores. Newsprint also comes in big sizes. It is sold at school supply stores, but, better yet, ask your local newspaper for some of their end runs. They often give this leftover paper away for free.

Chalkboards

My (aforementioned) affection for chalk pales in comparison to my fondness for chalkboards. Love 'em. And kids do too.

Chalkboards invite children to write. Each one is a literal blank slate, just waiting to be covered with a new idea.

Because they are so easily erased, chalkboards inherently encourage practice. Without a word, chalkboards suggest to kids, "Write something. Wipe it away. Write some more." How supportive!

Chalkboards also encourage learning in the opposite way: by offering resistance. As chalk drags across the board's rough surface, children get a "feel" for what they are writing. The feedback their little hands (and brains) receive from writing on a textured surface reinforces what they are seeing. In this way, writing on a chalkboard is a multisensory experience that really helps kids process the "big picture."

In addition to all that, I have to say that there is also something about the aesthetic of chalkboards that is just plain appealing. They have a classic, old-school look that evokes a sense of nostalgia. Although today's classrooms are getting equipped with the latest SMART Board technology, chalkboards are a timeless (and equally intelligent choice) for home.

DIY: Chalkboard Paint

Just imagine my delight when I discovered chalkboard paint. It was as if a new world had opened up to me! I painted one whole wall of my office, from floor to twelve-foot ceiling, in green chalkboard paint. And, oh, the writing that ensued!

At home, I've lost track of how many surfaces I've enhanced with chalkboard paint. I like to think of it as developmentally-appropriate décor. Wherever I find to use it, it turns a space into the perfect combination of form, function, and fun.

MATERIALS

painter's masking tape

chalkboard paint (available at hardware stores)

paintbrush

drop cloth

HOW-TO

1. Use low-tack painter's masking tape to section off the area you've chosen to be painted with chalkboard paint.
2. Following the directions on the paint can, apply a first coat of paint. Let it dry.
3. Repeat with one to two additional coats, allowing four to six hours' drying time between coats.
4. When paint is thoroughly dry, remove the masking tape.
5. Let the paint cure according to the directions, usually about two days.
6. Holding a piece of chalk on its side, rub the entire surface to cover it with a thin layer of chalk dust. Wipe off the excess.

Your chalkboard is now ready for use. You can write on it, erase it, and wash it with a barely damp cloth when needed. We use ours for drawing maps, leaving messages, writing to-dos, making special-occasion signs (like "Happy Birthday" and "Congratulations!"), keeping score, jotting down reminders, writing menus, and playing tic-tac-toe. We use it constantly; it was well worth the effort!

A Place of One's Own

As we learned from the movie *Field of Dreams,* if you build it, they will come. I assure you that this rule can apply in your home as well. If you make a place for it, they will write.

Devoting an area in your home to writing sends a message to your child. It says that writing is so important that it deserves its own special spot. It doesn't have to be an entire room of one's own, as writer Virginia Woolf described, just a dedicated area for organizing writing tools and supplies. Young writers will gravitate toward this spot to collect their materials and gather their thoughts. And they will know exactly where to find their latest work in progress when inspiration strikes.

FYI: Make Your Mark

Don't forget these other ingenious ideas:

- Tub crayons on bathtub walls
- Fabric markers on T-shirts
- Body crayons for messages on . . . you!
- Food markers for writing on your sandwich
- Magnetic letters on fridges, washers and dryers, little red wagons
- Window crayons on windows, glass doors, and mirrors
- Sidewalk chalk on the sidewalk, front steps, or a stone wall

My father built my first desk. I remember it clearly— it was blue with a pegboard back. And although it was kid-sized, it wasn't flimsy in the least. It was built like a battleship, which made me feel very important, as if he expected I would spend many hours there and that my work would be something to be reckoned with, a force of nature.

Carving out a little spot in your home for your young writers is more than just a way of saying, "Put your pencils here." It also communicates that you value their ideas. It's a promise to our kids that we are confident that the day will come when they will need to sit down and plot their course, draft their dreams, write their own story. Hey, childhood is the time to make big plans, you know? Creating a thoughtful corner for them to write it all down encourages them to find their own voices and to begin to carve out their own little niches in the world.

Desk and Chair

Remember Goldilocks? After eating up all that porridge, she felt a little tired and decided it would be a good idea to sit down. She passed up the first chair she tried (too hard), and turned her nose up at the second (too soft), but was pleased as punch with the third (just right). A girl after my own heart.

As parents, our most important job is to set our children up for success. And when it comes to writing, it is essential that we *seat* them for success as well. Like Goldilocks, our kids need the just-right chair in which to write. Not merely for comfort, the "just write" chair provides the best possible base of support.

The "just write" chair should help your child achieve the optimal posture for doing seated work at a table. How do you judge your child's posture? Look for three ninety-degree angles: a ninety-degree angle at the ankles with their feet flat on the floor, a ninety-degree angle at the knees; and a ninety-degree angle at the hips when your child's back is flat against the back of the chair.

What's the big deal? Well, think about writing in a moving vehicle. Have you ever tried it? First of all, it's quite challenging. Second of all, even if you do manage to accomplish the task, the end product is, let's just say, less than stellar. Without a stable base of support, it's nearly impossible to adequately control the movement of your hands. In other words, as I tell kids: when your body is wiggly, your writing will be wiggly too.

Everybody feels more stable and comfortable with their feet on the floor. It is terribly unsettling, not to mention uncomfortable, to sit in a too-big chair with your feet dangling in the air.

If children sit in oversized chairs, their instinct is to gain stability by sliding their hips forward and stretching out their legs so their feet touch the floor. This leads to a slouched posture. It also "locks" up their shoulders since they tend to push their upper bodies into the back of the chair in order to stay in the seat.

On the other hand, chairs that are too small for a child create their own problems. Children sitting in undersized chairs will find their knees up too high, making it difficult to get close enough to the table.

Once you find a chair that fits your child, take a look at the desk height. The rule of thumb is that a table should be approximately two inches higher than a child's bent elbow (when seated).

If a table is too low, children will have to slouch over to get their elbows near the table for support. When a table is too high, children raise their elbows and put them onto the table for support. (Hence the age-old "get your elbows off the table" complaint. Too bad generations of parents didn't realize their elbow-propping kids were just compensating for their small size in relation to a big table!)

Shelves, Drawers, and Cubbies

Writing is a process of self-discovery. It is the act of taking the thoughts stored in the recesses of your mind, sorting them out, and putting them on the page. Through writing, children find themselves. But before they can even get started, they first have to be able to find their stuff!

Believe it or not, there is a direct link between being able to access the ideas tucked away in your mind and being able to access your writing tools and materials. Since writing's inception, I wonder how many brilliant ideas have been lost forever whilst someone was rifling around for a stylus and a piece of papyrus (pencil and paper to you and me).

No matter how inspired an idea, it's not real until you write it down. Making sure young writers have the raw materials of their craft within reach is a surefire way to help them reach their learning potential. In other words, when the right writing tools are at a child's fingertips, learning will be well within their grasp.

That's where accessible storage comes in. Now we're not talking about storing anything major here. Say a jar of pencils, a tray of paper, a notepad, and a pencil sharpener for starters. These items should be kept at the ready beside your child's favorite writing spot. Other accoutrements can be stowed away in drawers, in cubbies, or on a nearby shelf—to be doled out as needed.

Want to make sure that an "all set to write and not a pencil in sight" situation doesn't happen in your home? Consider turning a spare cabinet into a writer's pantry, and you'll be sure to have all the essential ingredients for whatever writing project your kid cooks up.

Putting It All Together

Children's writing areas will need to develop along with them. Not only will they need chairs and desks that accommodate their growing bodies, they will also need the right tools and supplies to go along with their ever-improving skills. Like clothes that get worn out, outgrown, or phased out, a writing spot needs to be revamped periodically to make sure it still fits.

One Desk, Four Ways

Although hard to find, a height-adjustable desk and chair is a very sensible investment for a young writer (see the resources section at the end of the book). We fashioned my son's first desk from a piece of wood over two basic crates. The size was right, and it was pretty functional too. Then we organized his writing tools in the cubbies of an old chicken coop that was just his height. That's just one example of how creating a writing space is a good opportunity to be resourceful with what you have around the house. Think about size first. If you find a good fit, you can make it work.

After you fit, you must equip. For all ages there are some bare necessities: paper (white, lined, and maybe colored), pencils, crayons and markers, and a couple of notebooks. A chalkboard and chalk, a clipboard, scissors, tape, glue, and a stapler will also come in handy. With these basics kids are certainly off to a good start. Add a little something here or there as skills improve and interests change. The novelty will certainly pique their interest and may even inspire a brand new batch of ideas.

As far as setting it up, some suggestions according to the developmental stages follow.

For Scribblers

Scribblers, of course, can have the simplest desk space of all. Less is definitely more with our littlest ones.

First of all, too much stuff can be distracting. Young children may get sidetracked with dumping, sorting, or spreading everything all over the house. Secondly, things that pose a safety hazard—such as scissors, staplers, and a tape dispenser with a sharp cutting edge—should only be used with adult supervision and should not be left out. Lastly, if your children are so passionate about scribbling that they would love to redecorate the whole house, including walls and furniture, in the style of Early American Scribble, then stash crayons and markers out of reach until you're ready to keep a close eye on your avid young writers.

In fact, it's a good idea to store most of their gear in "eye's reach" but out of arm's reach (such as on a high shelf nearby). That way, little kids can see their tools and be inspired, and grown-ups can dole them out judiciously as needed. Think of it as encouraging them to choose from an appetite-whetting menu, as opposed to grabbing everything all at once from an irresistible self-serve buffet.

So what should be within reach? A short stack of plain white paper, definitely. White will offer the best contrast for those colorful scribbles, even if they are somewhat tentative. A compact tabletop easel (preferably with a chalkboard surface on one side) also makes a great addition to a Scribbler's desk. Consider adding a basket of alphabet stamps and a stamp pad—a great way for pre-writers to try their hand at adding letters to their work. And don't forget to make a clipboard available as well, for Scribblers on the go.

On the wall above the desk, how about hanging a poster of your child's name? You can print it simply, use numbered arrows, make textured letters, or coordinate it with your decor. Whatever suits. (Hint: always write your child's name with the first letter capitalized, and all the rest of the letters in lowercase.) This is hands-down the most important first word that Scribblers will learn to write; making an artful display of it will certainly inspire them (in signature style).

For Spellers

What do children who are working hard to learn how to write letters for the first time need on their desk? Plenty of paper, both white and colored. Plus a stack of three-by-five-inch index cards and a small three-by-five-inch chalkboard, the perfect size for practicing writing one letter at a time. And be sure to stock up on small, flip-top memo pads, a favorite among young Spellers everywhere.

Unlike Scribblers, Spellers can handle having all of their tools out and at the ready. A tool caddy is a great way to organize crayons, pencils, colored pencils, markers, glue, tape, and scissors. Try arranging tools in recycled jars on a lazy Susan, a repurposed silverware carryall, or a condiment holder. Anything that keeps them tidy and on-hand will work well.

As a parent of a Speller, there are times you might think to yourself, "If I had a dime for every time I heard 'How do I spell . . .' I'd be able to pay for their college education!" Yes, Spellers accumulate new words at a staggering rate. And all those words could use a tidy caddy of their own. Try using a basic rotating card file, such as a Rolodex, to organize your Speller's "word bank." As they learn or inquire about new words, write each one down on a card, file it alphabetically, and teach them how to flip and find to their hearts' content.

For over the desk, you can't beat hanging a print featuring the ABCs. The just-right combination of inspiration and information, an alphabet chart is the perfect visual to motivate your budding young writer.

For Storytellers

Welcome to the world of prolific printing. A Storyteller's desk must be set up accordingly. With paper galore. All shapes, sizes, and colors. Lined and unlined. Notebooks too. And don't forget lots and lots of drawing paper (see "Drawing Paper" in the templates section on page 205). Reams of it.

Book-making supplies are also a must. Store them all together in an available desk drawer. Include card stock for covers. Staplers, hole punchers, and string for binding. Labels for titles. And stickers, stamps, and stencils for embellishing.

Storytellers also make great letter writers. Designate another drawer for some social stationery (see "DIY: Letterhead" on page 43), greeting cards, envelopes, stamps, and an address book. Don't forget to add a small box for organizing incoming correspondence as well.

The perfect above-the-desk accompaniment to all of this storytelling is an inspiration board. Storytellers are chock full of ideas. In fact, they generate ideas even faster than they can generate stories. To organize all your Storyteller's ideas until their time comes, pin words, notes, pictures, and inspiring objects to a bulletin board over their desk. That way, when they sit down to write, they have to look no further than right in front of them for an idea to spark a story.

For Scholars

Scholars get down to serious business at their desks. Therefore, they require some serious tools. It's time for a dictionary and a thesaurus. An encyclopedia too. References worthy of promising wordsmiths. (Hint: we put a little red dot next to every word we look up in a reference book; I envision thousands of those dots covering the pages by the time my kids are college-bound.)

As for other materials, think outside the box. Keep your eye out for interesting items that will make scholarly writers feel like the real deal. Bound journals. Diaries. Logbooks. Legal pads. Graph paper. Ledger paper. Maybe even a fountain pen. The more grown-up it makes them feel, the better. Since we expect Scholars to respect the rules of writing, we can show them respect as well by trusting them with serious supplies.

The perfect solution for above a Scholar's desk is a great, big chalkboard or dry-erase board. It will act as mission control for them to organize and itemize all of their scholarly pursuits. If they think it, they can write it, right away. The ever-changing nature of the erasable board encourages them to make writing a daily habit. And when good writing habits are established from the get-go, they tend to last a lifetime. Write on!

A Writer's Pantry

I'm including a great big list of all the tools and supplies a budding writer could ever need. Rest assured, you really don't need *all* of these things, and you *certainly* don't need them all at once. You may pick stuff up here and there over time, repurpose some office supplies you already own, or grab a couple of things when you see them on sale. (Basic writing supplies make good little gifts too; a cute memo pad and decorative pencil is a no-brainer for stocking stuffers, goody bags, restaurant trips, or trick or treats.)

So here it is: a shopping list of the essential ingredients for a childhood's worth of writing fun.

Tools

* alphabet stampers
* chalk
* colored pencils
* crayons
* ink pad
* markers
* pencil grips
* pencils
* pens

Paper

* butcher paper
* card stock
* construction paper
* copy paper
* drawing paper
* kraft paper
* lined paper
* list paper
* newsprint
* poster board

STATIONERY

* blank labels
* blank tags
* envelopes
* folded cards
* handmade books
* index cards
* journals
* letterhead
* memo pads
* notebooks
* postcards
* stamps
* stationery
* sticky notes

SUPPLIES

* eraser
* glue
* glue stick
* hole punch
* magnetic letters
* paper clips
* pencil sharpener
* rubber bands
* ruler
* scissors
* sidewalk chalk
* stapler
* staples
* stickers
* string

REFERENCE

* address book or card file
* alphabet chart
* dictionary
* thesaurus

Make Yourself Write at Home

How to Encourage Your Budding Writer

I N THE INIMITABLE WORDS OF DOROTHY, "There's no place like home," especially where writing is concerned.

First smiles emerge when parents gaze lovingly into their baby's eyes. Wobbly first steps are taken while holding a parent's steady hand. And first words grow out of the back-and-forth babbling and banter shared by parent and child. So too should writing be learned one-on-one with a supportive parent.

Without a doubt, parents make the best first writing teachers. Parents are uniquely qualified to give emerging writers the loving attention and individualized instruction they thrive on. And, although teaching your child to write might not be entirely intuitive at first, it's easier than you may think. Especially now that you have some basic know-how, a bunch of great ideas about setup, and plenty of inspiration in the activities to follow.

Rest assured, the effort is well worth it. The rewards of raising a writer are abundant and far-reaching. As we have learned, strong writing skills pave the way for lifetime literacy, academic success, and love of learning.

There are other benefits as well. They take the form of little notes slid under doors, slipped into briefcases, and tucked under pillows. These scraps of paper document development in a way that a conversation, a phone call, an e-mail, or a text message can't. They are the bits and pieces of your child's life story.

The bottom line is this: every child has a story to tell, and that story begins at home.

Mamas and Papas Always Write

So now that you have an understanding of how writing skills develop, how you can prepare your children for writing, and how to set them up with the best tools, what else can you do to prioritize writing in your home? Well, that's simple . . . just write!

Children learn what they live. And one of the most effective ways to help a child learn something is by doing it yourself. When your children see you write every day, whether it's jotting down a shopping list, signing a check, or doing a crossword puzzle, they learn that writing is more than just a tool for school. It is a daily activity, a way of life.

Each day brings with it countless opportunities for you to be a writing role model. The simple act of saying out loud, "Oh! Let me write that down before I forget," demonstrates to children what I like to call the "writing reflex." *Think it, write it, remember it.* The more they see you do it, the more likely they will be to do it too. And the more they use their writing reflex, the stronger it will become. This is the stuff that good writing habits are built on. And once established, good writing habits last a lifetime.

Throughout the day, let your child "catch" you putting pen to paper for all sorts of interesting (and seemingly mundane) things. Invite them to join you, when you can. As they say, imitation is the sincerest form of flattery; don't be surprised if you see your child writing in a similar manner before you know it. Hey, maybe they'll even help you plow through that pile of paperwork on your desk (yeah, right!).

Writing Rituals

Many families have embraced the idea of reading to their children every day. Babies are read to before they have even begun to babble (some even while in the womb!). Preschoolers can listen to you read the repetitious rhymes and rhythms of colorful picture books for what seems like forever. Early readers follow along when captivating books are read to them, although they can't yet decipher all the words on their own.

We even ritualize reading by establishing certain times of the day and places in our home for reading. Bedtime stories fit snugly into the nighttime routine. Reading nooks are nestled into the corners of our houses. Books, often found in abundance, are proudly displayed on shelves and coffee tables. In many homes reading is learned in the lap. And children grow to appreciate it as a vital part of daily life.

But what about writing? What are the rituals that weave writing into the fabric of our families?

Like reading, writing should be tucked into the corners of every single day. Making writing a small part of the daily routine helps to create good writing habits. The simple act of putting pencil to paper with your child each day, no matter the reason, can make a big impact.

Think back to your own childhood, and try to remember what writing rituals went on in your home while you were growing up. In my home I remember there were letters to (and from) both Santa *and* the Tooth Fairy. I remember my mom putting signs on my bedroom door for special occasions, such as a big lightbulb-shaped poster that said, "You light up my life." I remember being my great-aunt Marion's "pen pal," writing thank-you notes to my father's business associate every time he gave us hockey tickets, getting love notes in my lunch bag, and exchanging messages with my family members each evening via a steamy shower door.

And how could I forget my little sister's sweet habit of sliding earnest notes of apology under my door every time I got angry at her for messing around with my stuff? It was quite endearing. (That is, until I found out she was writing all those notes with my lip liner. Ahem.)

Many families have little traditions that involve writing. Some parents write letters to their children each year on their birthday. Some keep scrapbooks or journals, full of milestones and memories. Others plan ahead, writing notes to their kids to be opened, one each day, when a parent is away on a trip. If you remember any rituals like these from your childhood that you want to continue with your kids, then definitely do your best to keep the tradition alive. If nothing like this rings a bell, then consider this your opportunity to invent a new "write" of passage in your home. Or do what I do, and strike a balance that feels right by combining a little of the old stuff with some new just-for-you rituals.

Sometimes a new writing ritual comes to you, out of the blue, inspired by current family events. For example, when my son was particularly discouraged over a perceived failure, I sat down and wrote a "Jack is . . ." list, itemizing all the qualities that make him especially lovable, capable, and successful. I read it to him, and then posted it in his room. As the days and weeks passed, I added more items to the list. And when he was able to identify a specific admirable quality of his own, he might suggest to me, "You should add that to 'the list'!" I often hear him reading the list to himself, especially when he goes to his room for some "thinking time" after a frustration or indiscretion. This is a small ritual that is a big reminder to us to label and record good, empowering feelings in writing, so they can be easily referred to when the going gets tough.

Simple yet sincere writing rituals can be slipped into your days with little extra effort. And just think, the rituals you pass on or invent today may become the traditions that your children will pass on to their own children tomorrow.

Here are some ideas for your own writing rituals:

> writing birthday letters
> creating a family newsletter to send out with holiday cards
> keeping a journal
> crafting a family memory book or scrapbook
> writing notes to be opened each day a parent is away on a trip
> putting a sign on a child's door on a special day
> making a certificate or award to commemorate an accomplishment
> writing a "My kid is . . ." list

Beyond Words

Even more important than our words, our actions as parents speak volumes. Budding writers look to our responses in their quest to be understood. With only a little more effort than it takes to hang a page on the refrigerator, we can display, preserve, share, and even publish our children's writing in ways that convey its great value. And (trust me on this) your kids will not only notice, they'll remember it forever.

Ideas for how to make your child feel like a full-fledged author can range from the simple to the spectacular. I once saw a musician on a reality show who brought his son to a tattoo parlor with him. The child wrote on his father's body using a magic marker, and his handwriting was turned into a one-of-a-kind tattoo for his dad. Totally extreme, I know.

Thankfully, there are many more accessible (and less painful) ways to honor your child's writing. Whatever you choose, the idea is to make young writers feel a little bit like rock stars themselves.

Display

Instead of adorning the walls of your home exclusively with famous artists' prints, try decorating with some "print" instead. My mom's got this one covered. There are little snippets of our writing framed around her house. Not only must it warm her heart to read and reread things like my second-grade composition about how well she took care of me on sick days, but it always gave me a kick to see it hanging there on the wall, for all the world to see. It made me feel as if my words mattered. For a child, that is a pretty powerful feeling. One that can be instrumental in motivating a child to write again and again.

How about a high-tech display of pride? A piece of your child's writing can make for an inspiring background or a screen saver for your computer.

Another way to display your child's writing is by being a walking billboard. (No, please don't put on one of those giant wearable sandwich signs. Your kid would never forgive you.) Simply print a piece of your child's writing onto iron-on transfer paper (see the resources section at the end of the book) and use it to embellish a T-shirt, tote bag, or baseball cap. When a boy that I had been working with learned to sign his name in cursive, I made him a custom logo T-shirt featuring his new-and-improved autograph. (It became his new signature T.)

Not extreme enough for you? I just remembered, you can turn your child's writing into a temporary tattoo using your own printer and specially formulated paper (see the resources section), an idea that's definitely all gain and no pain.

Share

Another wonderful way to honor your children's writing is by sharing it with others. You can make a piece of your child's writing into greeting cards simply by doing a little cutting and pasting. You can frame a piece of writing as a gift for a special relative or friend. You can use the iron-on transfer

DIY: Illuminated Manuscript

When you admire your children's bright ideas too much to file them away out of sight, try this cool candle-making project.

MATERIALS

blank paper

cylinder-shaped votive candleholder

pencil

scissors

computer and printer

translucent vellum printer paper

votive candle or tea light (for the flame phobic, LED battery-powered tea lights are an option)

double-stick tape

HOW-TO

1. Wrap a length of paper around a votive candleholder. Trim the paper so that the ends overlap approximately one inch. Using a pencil, trace along the top edge of the candleholder. Cut the paper along your line so that it is flush with the top of the candleholder. This will create a template.

2. Scan or photocopy a piece of your child's writing onto blank paper first. Adjust the size of the image to fit your template by reducing or enlarging it.

3. When you are happy with the size, print the image onto vellum printer paper following any specific printing instructions on the paper's package.

4. After the ink has dried (it takes longer for ink to dry on vellum than on regular paper), line up your candleholder template on the vellum paper, trace around it with a pencil, and cut out the vellum.

5. Wrap the vellum around your votive candleholder. Secure it at the seam, where the ends overlap, with double-stick tape.

6. When you're in the mood to feel "enlightened" by your child's words (or if you are looking for a heartfelt gift idea), insert a candle and enjoy.

technique I mentioned to make all sorts of wearable gifts. You can make a keepsake-worthy gift by decorating a plain wooden box with a piece of your child's writing and sealing it with a clear decoupage medium such as Mod Podge; it will last for years. Another idea is to embellish the cover of a blank journal with a piece of your child's writing, making a gift that is both sentimental and useful. (Oh, and maybe it goes without saying, but these all make A+ teacher gifts as well.)

If you are particularly creative you could turn a piece of writing into a lasting memento by embroidering it onto cloth. Then you could frame it, make into a pillow, or incorporate it into a quilt. In the olden days, this was the idea behind the samplers that became both family treasure and valuable folk art. My needlework skills aren't quite there yet, but maybe someday! (Although this one might be difficult to give away as a gift once complete. For me, it might be more of a *keep*sake.)

Preserve

You don't have to work for the Library of Congress or the Smithsonian to be an archivist. You just have to be a parent. Take myself, for example. I'm a keeper. I've saved just about every piece of paper my kids have made a mark on. Someday, I'm sure I'll weed through it. For now, those pages document our journey along the road to writing. To me, they're priceless papers.

So how do you organize the keeping? Use simple systems.

File: Filing is probably the easiest method of keeping papers. Just slip the pages you want to save into a file folder. It's easy to manage in the moment, easy to flip through and find something later on.

Box: Repurpose an empty shirt box, unused pizza box, or oversized shoebox into an archival box. Toss in your children's pages without any additional fuss as they accumulate. Once or twice a year, sort through the stack, removing anything you can bear to part with.

Binder: We use a lot of three-ring binders with sheet protectors around here. It's really the perfect solution for keeping drawings, pages of a story, lists, poems, and other writing all together and ready to be flipped through at any time. It's easy, organized, and very functional.

Digital archive: Are you inundated with paper pileup? Put technology on your side. Simply scan what you want to store, and save it on your computer. Then toss the hard copies guilt-free.

Scrapbook: Create a scrapbook devoted to your kids' writing, or incorporate their handwritten snippets and stories in more traditional scrapbook layouts.

Bound book: These days, the opportunities to self-publish are plentiful (some of these sites are listed in the resources section at the end of the book). The process has become very user-friendly and the product is quite impressive. And remember, all the photo book-making sites (see the resources section) can also accommodate uploading scanned images of your child's writing. So when you have collected some words or stories worth saving forever in a high-quality medium, what could be better than a bound book?

Publish

Quite possibly, the ultimate affirmation for a young writer (or any writer, for that matter) is getting published. There are dozens of websites, a handful of print magazines, and a few anthologies that accept and publish submissions from young writers. (I've listed a few publishing opportunities for children in the resources section at the end of the book.)

Certainly there is a strong sense of satisfaction when you pull a publication off a newsstand or a book off a shelf and see your words in print. But it goes beyond that. Being published can have a profound effect on a young writer's self-esteem. Writers need readers. When young writers realize they can connect to a wider audience, they begin to realize the far-reaching power of the written word.

Note to Self

In short, I will sum up what I've seen parents do that has worked and that I am trying my best to emulate in my own home. Consider it a concise yet vigorous manifesto for raising a writer.

Provide support. Create opportunities to write. Admire and appreciate. *Read every word*. Save, share, and show off writing samples. Equip a writing space. Keep necessary tools on hand. Let your kids catch you in the act of writing. Often. Write with your kids every day (even the small stuff matters). Every so often, say the words "once upon a time." Don't stop talking until you reach "the end." Read, read, read. Together, read everything you can get your hands on, not just stories. Newspapers, magazines, correspondence, flyers, manuals, road signs, cereal boxes—whatever piques your child's interest. If they write to you, write back. Write them love notes. Sign them with *X*s and *O*s. Carry a pencil and paper with you, wherever you go. Say, "That's something worth writing about!" so often that your kids say it in their sleep.

What shouldn't we do? Avoid editing our kids' writing. Avoid it like the plague. Especially during the early stages of writing development, avoid correcting, critiquing, or changing their writing in any way. Unless they ask for specific help, stand back and give them some room to figure it out on their own before rushing in to save the day. Put the red pen away. There will be plenty of time for all that stuff once writing is well established. For now, our job is to raise kids who love to write. The best way to do that is to show them that we love their writing.

And in that spirit, I encourage you to enjoy the fifty-two activities that follow. Think of each one as a unique opportunity to invite the fun of writing into your home and the love of writing into your child's life.

Guidelines for the Activities

THE FIFTY-TWO "Just Write" activities in the next section are writing activities that provide the just-right challenge for kids—they are motivating for children, requiring them to slightly stretch their skills, yet without being too difficult. You know you're on the right track when kids get that "I can do it!" look on their faces. When children master something, everything changes. You can see it in their posture (they sit up a little taller), in their attention (they stick with it and want to do more, more, more!), and in their self-esteem (you know those "Hey! Look at me!" moments).

Each activity features four variations to help you achieve the just-right fit for your child. In addition, a few simple guidelines will set your kids up for success:

Mind the grasp: If a child is using an inefficient grasp, you want to modify the tool (a smaller writing tool, such as a broken crayon, may help), modify the grasp (demonstrate an efficient grasp or provide a pencil picture, for example), or modify the activity (they may need to back up to a more basic variation). What you don't want to do is reinforce an inefficient grasp by encouraging your child to keep writing. Remember the rule: don't write until it's right.

Pay attention to their attention: If children rush through an activity or quickly lose interest, it may be too easy. If their attention wanders and they need constant refocusing, it may be too hard.

Fend off frustration: Frustration is another sign that an activity is too difficult. Step in to help if you see signs of struggle.

Watch for signs of fatigue: Some common signs of fatigue are a slouched posture, holding their heads in their hands, switching the writing tool from one hand to another, or complaining of hand pain. If you see any of these, it's definitely time to take a break.

Remember to seat for success: Don't forget to sit your children where they fit, and get them in the right position by reinforcing stomp, slide, slant, and slap.

Organized materials encourage organized work: Kids have a natural tendency to place their paper on top of a big pile of clutter and start working with complete disregard for the disorder. Help them get into the habit of clearing the decks (or their desks) before they get to work.

Remember you're here to help: When you nurture your children's writing skills at home, consider them to be your apprentices. Have patience when demonstrating an activity, and whenever possible, teach by modeling.

Keep expectations realistic: Newbie writers need plenty of time to practice the process before they can perfect the product. Look for progress, not perfection.

Make it playful: At the heart of all these activities is the idea that children who play with writing, in a variety of ways, will not only learn to write, but will learn to love writing.

And, just like that, they're ready to write.

52 "Just Write" Activities

Learn

Whether children are Scribblers ready for the next step, Spellers forming letters, Storytellers honing their craft, or Scholars learning cursive, the activities in this next section will help you to help them.

These hands-on, multisensory learning experiences go way beyond tracing, copying, or worksheet-type tasks. Each one is designed with development in mind. They support writing success by involving all the senses, incorporating big movements and small movements, and combining cognitive and motor components. Most important, they facilitate foundational skills by focusing on the building blocks of fluent, automatic, stress-free writing. And did I mention that they're fabulously fun and kid-friendly too? And that's no small thing. Because when kids learn to love writing from the start, well, that's something that lasts a lifetime.

1

Skywriting

OOK UP IN THE SKY! It's a bird... it's a plane... no, it's a plane that knows how to write!

When you see skywriting, it really grabs your attention. The novelty of those puffy white letters against a backdrop of endless blue sky heightens your awareness and makes you stop and take notice.

Your children can try their own hands at "skywriting" as they're learning to write, by pretending their hands are airplanes that are writing giant letters in the air. Introduce them to this idea by standing alongside them and demonstrating a letter movement in the air, using big motions of your entire arm. Encourage them to do the same. A funny thing happens when they "write" using large, whole-body movements: their brain really stops and takes notice. How so? Big movements activate more areas of the brain, thus reinforcing the information at hand. By practicing letter formation with super-sized movements first, learning virtually takes flight.

Oh, and don't forget to make some good airplane noises, too, to enhance the high-flying fun. Enjoy doing this one together, knowing that once children feel comfortable enough to fly solo, the sky's the limit.

MATERIALS

* None! Just you and your young writer.

How-to

Stand side-by-side with your child and trace the movements of various letters of the alphabet in the air using the largest motions you can. Say the directions out loud at first ("Zoom straight down, fly back to the top, and make a great big curve" for capital *D,* for example), and then fade them out as your child masters the movements.

Variations

For Scribblers: Start with letter strokes (lines and curves) and basic shapes (circles, squares, and triangles), rather than entire letters. Getting your children used to controlling the movement of specific shapes will help them develop the control needed to form letters.

For Spellers: Demonstrate the ABCs as described; Spellers are ready for this. When demonstrating the letters, be sure to form them using the proper stroke order (see "Alphabet Chart" in the templates section on page 203).

For Storytellers: As children progress, they're ready to tackle some simple words. Encourage your Storyteller to test out their newly learned words in the sky.

For Scholars: This is a super multisensory way for Scholars to practice spelling words or writing letters in cursive. To help Scholars focus on the feel of words even more, try having them close their eyes while they skywrite (it helps them to really home in on the direction of their movements).

2

What's in the Bag?

HAVE YOU EVER HEARD anyone say, "You're so good at that, I bet you could do it with your eyes closed"? They would be referring to the fact that once you have learned something in a multisensory way, your inner awareness of how to do it is so strong you could easily do it with your vision occluded. That's exactly how we want to teach children to write letters. We want their hands to be guided by their internal sense of each letter's movement so that their writing flows automatically.

The best way for children to get a feel for letters is by actually *feeling* them. Picking them up in their hands, manipulating them, running their fingers along their lines and curves. When they do this, they are able to see them in their "mind's eye." Then, they are better able to visualize how to make the letters themselves.

This game reinforces that concept. And you'll be surprised at how much concentration it takes; it's not as easy as it looks!

MATERIALS

* a full set of three-dimensional alphabet manipulatives (such as alphabet puzzle pieces, or magnetic alphabet letters)
* medium-sized opaque drawstring bag
* blindfold or handkerchief (optional)

How-to

1. Put the alphabet letters in the bag and pull the drawstring snug.
2. Show your kids how to loosen the drawstring, then shut their eyes and slip one hand into the bag. (No peeking! You might have to use a blindfold for persistent peekers.)
3. Tell them to identify something in the bag using only their sense of touch. Have them say what they think it is out loud *before* they pull it out of the bag.
4. Kids can double-check themselves by pulling out the letter and seeing whether they got it right (if they did, keep the letter out of the bag and try some others). If they didn't get it right, they can put the letter back in and try it again on another turn.

Variations

For Scribblers: Even Scribblers who don't know their letters yet can start learning to tune in to their sense of touch. Start by putting a few simple objects (like a key, a ball, a crayon, a shell, or a spoon) into the bag and see if they can identify the items without looking at them.

For Spellers: Kids who are just learning their letters will love this game, provided you take their novice status into account. Start out by placing only two letters in the bag at a time. Choose letters that they know well and that have dissimilar shapes (A and O, for example). Follow the instructions as described above. As a variation, make a specific request, such as, "Find the A."

For Storytellers: Hide letters in the bag that, when combined, spell a simple word your Storyteller knows well. Have them reach in, feel, and guess each letter. When they have figured out all the letters and taken them out of the bag, encourage them to arrange and rearrange them until they discover the secret word.

For Scholars: Scholars are ready for a challenge. Toss all twenty-six letters into the bag and let them rummage about until they find one they can identify. You can even turn this into a game with several players. Each player reaches into the bag and tries to feel and find a letter. If they get it right, they keep the letter. If they mistake one letter for another, they place it back in the bag. The bag gets passed from one player to the next until there are no more letters left inside. The player who has accumulated the most letters by the end of the game is the winner.

3

Mystery Letters

"WRITING" letters on kids' backs is another one of those activities that help them visualize letter formation without the help of their visual sense. (Unless your child is a Cirque du Soleil wannabe, it's pretty much impossible for them to peek at what you're writing back there.) It's therefore an ideal activity for facilitating that internal awareness of letter formation. In my house, we have also found it to be an ideal activity for bedtime, when the lights are turned down anyway and the soft touch and quiet nature of this activity invites both concentration and calm.

MATERIALS

* None! Just a quiet spot.

HOW-TO

Simply trace a letter of the alphabet on your child's back and wait to see if he or she can guess the letter. If your child can't identify the letter, try it one or two more times before revealing the mystery letter. Start with capital letters first, because they have simpler shapes. When your child has mastered all the capitals, you can introduce lowercase letters.

Variations

For Scribblers: When you're first starting out, just alternate between writing two distinctly different letters (like *X* and *O*) and see whether your children can differentiate one from the other.

For Spellers: Try writing a few familiar letters on their backs (such as the letters in their names) and see if they can identify them.

For Storytellers: Work your way up to including all the letters of the alphabet and finally words and little messages, such as "sweet dreams" and "I love you" (using a pat on the back to indicate a space between words).

For Scholars: This is a fun and motivating way for Scholars to review spelling or vocabulary words. It's especially effective at bedtime, as the mind tends to rehearse and retain the information it processed right before it went to sleep.

4

A-B-Centerpiece

GROWING UP, during large family meals at Grandma's house, we kids were not put at a kiddie table (though the idea was mentioned quite a bit). Instead we sat with the grownups, until long after we finished eating and had lost interest in the adult conversation.

What kept us all at the table? And relatively quiet? A magnetic letter board scrounged from Grandma's half-empty toy box. Although many of the letters were missing, we spelled out silly messages to each other, often improvising by substituting one letter for another (a *Z* on its side can stand in for an *N* in a pinch, for example) or inventing creative spellings.

Believe it or not, this tradition continued into our young adulthood—our messages becoming cleverer using our college-level vocabulary. We even brought dinner dates to the table and inaugurated them into our silly word play.

Inspired by those gatherings at Grandma's house, I made sure to incorporate a hands-on alphabet into my own family's mealtime routine early on. You never know what will be spelled out at our table: names, food requests, dinner reviews (although I plead ignorance if anyone asks me how to spell "yuk"). There's even the occasional silly sentiment, to remind me of the good old days at Grandma's.

MATERIALS

* a full set of three-dimensional alphabet manipulatives (such as alphabet puzzle pieces, magnetic alphabet letters, alphabet blocks, Scrabble tiles, dry alphabet pasta, or alphabet beads)

HOW-TO

1. Set out the alphabet letters in an appropriate container in the middle of your table for your kids to discover.
2. Model using the letters by spelling out messages to your kids (such as, "Good morning kiddo!" or "Eat your veggies"), and then read and reinforce any messages they write back.

Variations

For Scribblers: For the littlest letter-learners, put a bowl of alphabet puzzle pieces (one of each letter) in the middle of the table. Encourage them to pick up the letters one at a time and "try out" the sound, or match them up to objects ("*B* is for banana"). Help your child to start identifying the different letters.

For Spellers: Children who are more familiar with letters and are starting to combine them to make words need more letters to work with. A basket of alphabet blocks helps children start to "build" their ideas.

For Storytellers: For children who are stringing their thoughts together into sentences, try setting out a dish of magnetic alphabet letters and a cookie sheet.

For Scholars: Interesting alphabet letters can motivate older children to practice their spelling words at the table. Try setting out a candy dish full of small, dry alphabet pasta; a trifle dish full of Scrabble tiles; or a plate full of alphabet beads and laces.

And here's a little ABC 411, FYI. Did you know that the most frequently used alphabet letters are: *E, T, A, I, N, O,* and *S*? Make sure you have some extras of these letters on hand!

5

A-maze-ing You

WHETHER YOU'RE TEACHING a child how to hold a pencil for the first time, helping an emerging writer improve an awkward grip, or encouraging young writers-in-residence to refine their grasps (for increased legibility, speed, and endurance), mazes provide great pencil-holding practice. Think of mazes as driver's ed for little hands. Staying on track, following the lines and curves, and planning ahead are as good exercises in motor control as you can get—and a great workout for children at every writing stage.

I prefer mazes to be of the homemade variety, able to be personalized on a whim. I make a simple drawing (no artistic skill required here, I'm talking stick figures and basic shapes) at the upper left-hand corner of the page, and then another at the bottom right-hand corner. (Whatever my son is interested in at the moment inspires the starting point and the destination. It may be a race car and a finish line, a rocket ship and a moon, a little boy and an ice cream cone; you get the idea.) Then I draw a labyrinth of lines back and forth across the page from the starting point to the goal. This never fails to amuse and occupy. In fact, it is the perfect activity for down time in restaurants, doctors' office waiting rooms, or (gasp) the Department of Motor Vehicles (think of it as a mini road test!).

* paper
* pencil, crayons, or markers

How-to

1. Draw a maze on a piece of paper, then hand it over for your child to complete. Ask for some kid input when creating the challenge to motivate your little problem solver.

Variations

For Scribblers: The first strokes that pre-writers will master are simple vertical and horizontal ones. Mazes should be as basic as possible, say a simple straight path from a car to a garage, or from a bumblebee to a flower. The challenge here is for little fingers to guide a pencil to stay between the lines (which should be at least an inch apart) without veering off course.

For Spellers: Emerging writers can be challenged with lines that are closer together (about one-half inch apart) and that switch directions (back and forth and up and down).

For Storytellers: Children who have had some more pencil-holding experience are ready to tackle narrow lines, twists and turns, obstructions, and dead ends (which require them to retrace their lines in order to "turn around").

For Scholars: More complex mazes resemble mini paper-and-pencil obstacle courses and can even incorporate some written directions, such as: "Zigzag back and forth through the flags," "Loop around each rock three times," or "Travel down this path using a wavy line." Game on!

6

Sand Writing

CAN'T THINK of any better way for young writers to hone their letter formation skills than to write with their fingers in sand. The surface area of a fingertip contains an extremely large concentration of tactile receptors, each one sending a message to children's brains as they write. Sand makes all of those tiny little receptors positively hum with rich information.

And while sand writing is an ideal activity to do in a sandbox or at the beach (with the waves as Mother Nature's eraser), an excursion is not required. Sand writing is just as engaging when done at the kitchen table or in the playroom. When you set this up, be ready to stay put for a while, though. Running your fingers through the sand is rather habit forming, and children love to explore this reinforcing (and relaxing) activity for what may seem like an eternity.

MATERIALS

* shallow box or tray
* about one to two cups of sand (cornmeal works too)
* broom and dustpan (optional, but advised)

How-to

1. Fill the box or tray with about one-fourth to one-half inch of clean sand.
2. Show your children how to make shapes, trace letters, and write words in the sand.
3. Demonstrate how to "erase" the writing by smoothing out the sand with a flat hand.
4. Read and reinforce any writing your children want to share with you.

Variations

For Scribblers: Start with vertical and horizontal strokes, simple shapes, or lines with repeating patterns (such as waves, loops, or zigzags).

For Spellers: Practice one letter at a time over and over by playing "disappearing letter." Act surprised when your child makes a letter vanish, saying, "Where on earth did that *E* go? It was just there! Can you find it?" Feign shock and amazement when they re-create it, as if by magic.

For Storytellers: Your Storyteller may love having two trays, side by side, one to draw in and one in which to write a word that corresponds to their picture.

For Scholars: More spelling words to practice for homework tonight? Ditch the drudgery, and pull out the sand tray instead.

7

Letters 'R' Us

NOWADAYS, kids are becoming savvy shoppers at a young age. They know all about swiping credit cards, signing receipts, and using coupons. And it intrigues them. So much so that, every time I introduce kids to this activity, they become quite the shopaholics. They love being the ones to mind the store (especially when there's a cool cash register involved).

In this project, have your kids set up a letter store. Would you like to buy an *E*? How about all the letters to spell your name? With twenty-six letters in stock, the possibilities are unlimited. And with play money, kisses, and hugs for currency, the price is definitely right.

MATERIALS

* letter pieces (wood pieces for capital letters available from Handwriting Without Tears, or you can make your own using a template, also available from Handwriting Without Tears; see the resources section at the back of the book)
* puppet theater (or trifold presentation board, available at office supply stores)
* cutting knife (if using a presentation board)
* toy cash register

* play money
* small paper shopping bag
* scrap paper
* pencil

How-to

1. Help your children set up their inventory of letter pieces behind a storefront. A puppet theater works great as a storefront, if you have one. If you don't, you can create a super-simple shop by cutting a rectangular opening in the middle panel of a piece of trifold presentation board (grown-ups only for this cutting job, please). Children can decorate the facade or write the name of their store on it.

2. Set up the cash register, play money, shopping bag, scrap paper, and pencil, so they are all accessible.

3. Parents, have fun being your kids' customers. Play the part to the hilt. I usually say something to the effect of, "Excuse me sir/ma'am. I'm looking for a letter. It's a f-f-fabulous letter. It's made up of a big straight line and two little straight lines. Do you have anything like that in stock?"

4. Your little shopkeeper can then scurry around putting your order together, placing the pieces in your bag, ringing you up, taking your money, giving you back your change, and writing you a receipt.

5. Check your order when you get your bag, and if it's not exactly what you asked for, cheerily repeat your request and ask for an exchange.

6. Model gracious thank-yous and have-a-nice-days at the end of your transaction. Kids eat it up. They'll want to play over and over again. Who doesn't want repeat customers?

Variations

For Scribblers: Since they are just getting comfortable with lines and shapes, start there with your requests. Begin by ordering a big straight line, and, if they master that, order a big curve next, and so on.

For Spellers: Spellers thrive on the transaction I quoted above; it's right where they're at, developmentally speaking. When they have mastered finding letter pieces and can identify all the letters, I might up the challenge by saying, "I am looking for the first letter of the word *fish*."

For Storytellers: Step it up another notch for Storytellers because they can definitely serve you up an entire word (for example, "Could you please sell me everything I need to make *fish* for dinner?").

For Scholars: Use the definition of a word in your order, such as "an aquatic animal with gills," and your young Scholar will hardly be able to guess they are studying vocabulary *and* spelling as they play.

8

Eat Your Words

SERVING KIDS an edible alphabet is a delicious way to whet their appetites for writing. When my son was just learning letters, I was known to dish up eggs that spelled J-A-C-K, pancakes that implored "Eat," and pasta that asked "How are you?" Now, following my lead, he makes alphabet cookies and creates words out of pretzel dough. Hey, in our house it might not be okay to *play* with your food, but if you're going to *write* with it, well, that's another story.

MATERIALS

* food items, such as pancake batter, cookie dough, cheese slices, pretzel dough, alphabet pasta, or spaghetti
* cooking tools, such as alphabet cookie cutters

HOW-TO

Experiment with food presentations that incorporate alphabet shapes. Some suggestions follow.

Variations

For Scribblers: Pre-writers will certainly enjoy eating a plate full of ABCs. Try using a squeeze bottle or turkey baster to carefully squirt pancake batter onto your skillet in the shape of alphabet letters. If you are truly talented, write the letters backward (the flip side always comes out better).

For Spellers: New writers love cutting out cookie dough, and almost anything else, with alphabet cookie cutters. (Try also cutting cheese slices, fried eggs, sandwiches, toast, or tortillas.) The cookie cutters allow Spellers to select specific letters to work with so they can form an edible word. Y-U-M!

For Storytellers: Storytellers can form letter shapes on their own, by rolling out pretzel, cookie, pizza, or bread dough into long snakes. Have them shape the dough into letter shapes, bake, and eat! Will they be able to resist the temptation to eat their letters long enough to form an entire sentence? Well, that's another tale.

For Scholars: Spaghetti for your thoughts? Alphabet macaroni (or oh-so-shapeable spaghetti) can be used to write out oodles of ideas.

9

Alphabox

WHEN PRESENTED WITH A BOX, most people respond in one of two ways. There are the box shakers, who rattle, turn, and examine the box, hoping to glean a clue to its contents. And there are those who relish the imminent surprise.

Most kids fall in the curious category when it comes to boxes with unknown contents. Hence the appeal of the alphabox. The concept is simple: sneak an interesting object into a box, place the box where it will be discovered, and wait for inquisitive kids to peek inside. (You won't have to wait long; it's just plain irresistible.)

Once they've taken a look at the contents, challenge them to write the starting sound or the name of the object on the top of the box. Not only are they learning to use symbols to represent objects (one of the most basic tenets of writing), but they are also practicing their writing skills as they play along.

MATERIALS

* sturdy box with a lid that closes
* chalkboard paint
* interesting objects
* chalk

How-to:

1. Paint the top of the box with chalkboard paint.
2. When the box is dry, hide an interesting object in it and leave it somewhere where your child will stumble upon it.
3. When the box is found, tell your child to write the first letter of the name of the secret object on the top of the box.
4. If they guess right, replace the secret object with another one, hide the box somewhere else, and watch the fun continue.

Variations

For Scribblers: Stick to hiding objects with simple shapes (such as a pencil, ball, or block) in the box, and have your pre-writers draw the shape they discover.

For Spellers: The ability to identify starting sounds is an essential skill for emerging writers. Put familiar objects in the box first, and then proceed to more challenging objects.

For Storytellers: Encourage Storytellers to write the entire name of the secret object.

For Scholars: Up the ante by daring more confident writers to take a guess at the item in the box without peeking. Give them some cryptic clues, and, after they write their guess, let them open the box to see how they did.

10

Luck of the Draw

ALL WRITING EVOLVES from drawing. While drawing, children experiment with the lines, curves, and shapes that they will soon use to make letters. They develop and refine their grasp of various writing tools. They learn to coordinate their eyes with their hands as they doodle, color, and sketch. They learn to tell stories with images. And they learn that if they can envision something, they can make it a reality on the page.

Because it builds creativity, control, coordination, and confidence, drawing should be encouraged at home. Motivate your children to draw often and with enthusiasm by setting an example. Don't be self-conscious about your drawing skills—the product doesn't matter, it's the process that counts. Stick figures are welcome here. Get the picture?

MATERIALS

* colored pencils, crayons, markers, or a graphite pencil
* plain paper or drawing paper (see "Drawing Paper" in the templates section on page 205)

How-to

1. Set aside a special time for drawing on a regular basis. Grab some colorful writing tools and a stack of paper and gather around the table to illustrate some of your brightest ideas.
2. Share your drawings with each other and display them somewhere you can admire them.

Variations

For Scribblers: When you draw alongside Scribblers, think abstract expressionism rather than realism. What I mean is, don't draw what they can't. It frustrates them and makes them question their abilities. Instead, channel your own inner Scribbler. Cover your paper with bright colors and broad strokes. You'll probably find it's even more fun than you remember.

For Spellers: Introduce emerging writers to the concept that artists sign their work. When they finish a drawing, direct them to put their signatures in the corner, a habit almost as valuable as the art itself.

For Storytellers: Storytellers are ready for drawing paper, which is paper that has blank space at the top (for a picture) and lines at the bottom (for words). Here is where children become author-illustrators, and the words and the pictures become complementary to one another.

For Scholars: Because Scholars have big ideas, they can branch out to more detailed drawings. Think: comic strips, storyboards, blueprints, shop drawings, charts, maps, and diagrams.

Make

Whether children are Scribblers ready for the next step, Spellers forming letters, Storytellers honing their craft, or Scholars learning cursive, the activities in this next section will help you to help them.

Any time you help your children to craft something that encourages writing, be prepared to be amazed by the results. Kids that know how to create their own writing-based tools tend to use them for their intended purpose. Often. And that means plenty of writing will follow. On top of that, making stuff that requires writing—such as signs and newspapers—teaches children that, when it comes to being a creative writer, the sky's the limit. Don't be surprised if they start coming up with their own inventive ideas. Begin by introducing your kids to the activities in the next section. Resourceful young writers will be able to take it from there.

11

Air Mail

LOOKING FOR THE PERFECT WAY to help your children's writing skills take off? Just show them how to send messages via airmail (aka turning notes into paper airplanes), and watch their enthusiasm for writing soar.

Making paper airplanes is a classic childhood pursuit. Turning messages into airplanes, however, takes the fun to a whole new level. What can be better than seeing your thoughts (literally) take flight? Now that's a special delivery!

Plain or ruled paper works great for this activity. Have a stack at the ready, because once kids catch on, they tend to become frequent flyers. This is also a fantastic activity for your children to do with a buddy—jetting messages back and forth is even more fun with a friend.

An added bonus of airmail? All that folding really helps build kids' fine motor skills. And that's really something to write home about!

MATERIALS

* a piece of standard 8½ × 11 inch paper
* writing tool of choice

How-to

Show kids how to turn a letter-sized page of their writing into a paper airplane following these instructions.

1. Fold the paper in half lengthwise to create a line down the center. Then unfold it.
2. Fold the top two corners down to meet the center line, creating a triangle at the top of the paper.
3. Fold the top part of the triangle down so that the point of the triangle meets the center crease about one inch above the bottom of the paper.
4. Fold the new top corners down to meet the center line as you did before. There should be a little triangle peeking out from below the new top triangle.
5. Fold your paper along the center line in the opposite direction of your original fold.
6. Fold each diagonal edge of the paper down so that it meets the edge with the center fold. Unfold these "wings" slightly.
7. Holding the plane by its center fold, point the nose up in the air, and lett-er rip!

Variations

For Scribblers: Pre-writers will be delighted to see their colorful scribbles or drawings coast through the air. They may need some help planning and lining up the folds, but be sure to leave them in charge of creasing the paper.

For Spellers: The only thing that tops learning to write a new word is sending your hard work soaring through the air to be caught and admired.

For Storytellers: Young writers will really appreciate learning a new way to send all those messages they are so eager to write, such as "Can I go out and play now?" and "What's for dinner?"

For Scholars: If you want to get your child geared up to study for that spelling test, this is a sure thing. Have your child write out the words and then fly them over to you for correction.

12

All the News

EXTRA, EXTRA, write all about it!

Do your kids realize that every day is full of newsworthy events? Maybe they scored a goal in a soccer game or got a good grade on a test. Perhaps someone learned to pump a swing or tied shoelaces for the first time. Did the next-door neighbor have a bumper crop of tomatoes or grow a particularly enormous gourd? Are they repaving Main Street, renovating the movie theater, or painting the playground equipment? Inquiring minds want to know.

New and noteworthy stuff is happening from minute to minute. Just encourage your kids to consider it all grist for the newspaper-writing mill. Then kick back, and enjoy reading it with your cup of morning joe.

MATERIALS

* blank newsprint paper (or other large paper)
* alphabet stampers and ink pad
* pencil
* black marker

How-to

1. Look at a real newspaper with your kids, pointing out relevant details and discussing where and how reporters find their stories and get their facts.
2. Show your kids how to conduct a simple interview, compose an attention-grabbing headline, write a simple article, and lay out a newspaper page.

Variations

For Scribblers: Encourage Scribblers to get in touch with their inner printing press. Using alphabet stampers, they can "typeset" all over their piece of newsprint, strengthening fine motor (and letter identification) skills as they go.

For Spellers: Introduce Spellers to the idea of a press release, so they can broadcast important news items in writing, such as "Jack lost a tooth" or "Gracie said 'Mama.'"

For Storytellers: Storytellers are ready to learn about the *W*s (plus one *H*) of a good news story: Who? What? When? Where? Why? and How? They can use an article-writing worksheet (see "Article Writing Worksheet" in the templates section on page 206) to organize their information.

For Scholars: Challenge Scholars to learn and use the parts of a real newspaper layout (see "Parts of a Newspaper" in the templates section on page 207).

13

Signs

IGNS ARE A SIMPLE yet effective way for children to make their mind known. In fact, while I was writing this, my son asked for some help making a "No Mommies Allowed" sign for his clubhouse. I obliged (slightly begrudgingly).

Signs come in all shapes and sizes. There are billboards and neon signs for the flamboyant among us. And a simple sticky note on the bathroom mirror suffices for the discreet. In between, there are banners, dry-erase and chalkboard signs, signs made from poster board, and signs that hang on doorknobs. Whether subtle or sensational, signs are aimed to catch the eye of a passerby and say, "Look-y here. This is the deal."

And don't worry too much if you get some "Do Not Enter (Or Else!)" signs every now and then. At a certain age, kids start needing a little personal space. Just consider it a sign of the times.

MATERIALS

* poster board, cardboard, card stock, sticky notes, butcher paper, doorknob sign (see "Doorknob Sign" in the templates section on page 208), or paper
* crayons, pens, pencils, magic markers
* tape

How-to

1. Encourage children to speak their minds with signs. When it comes to the design, remember these rules:
    * Keep it simple: if there is too much visual clutter, the sign will be hard to read.
    * Use eye-catching colors: entice the eyes to stop and look.
    * Use big, bold lettering: write for readability (unless, of course, your message includes some "fine print").
2. Show children how to post signs where their target audience is most likely to see them.

Variations

For Scribblers: Make a big sign, such as "Happy Birthday, Dad," with block letters (outlined only). Have your Scribbler help color in each letter. This is a great way to introduce and review letter recognition with your Scribbler.

For Spellers: The world's best signs are short and to the point (think: "Stop," "Open/Closed," "Exit," "Wet Paint"). These kinds of signs are just right for Spellers.

For Storytellers: Storytellers usually have a lot to say. Poster board (in lieu of a billboard by the highway) is a good choice for effusive signage, such as the rules to a made-up game or elaborate instructions for entering a room.

For Scholars: When it was homework time at my house, my older sister and I used to have "Battle of the Signs." Hers would read, "Quiet Study Section" and mine, "Noisy Sister Section." Doorknob signs are a great way for Scholars to communicate whether they're having a "Do Not Disturb" moment or a "Come In and Hang Out" one.

14

Handmade Books

THERE IS ONLY ONE THING you need to turn a young writer into an author: a book.

Handmade books are great to have on hand for when book-worthy inspiration strikes. Easy to make, they're just as easy to fill up with ideas. From cover to cover, children can let their imaginations run wild.

And speaking of covers, here's an opportunity to get really creative. While colored card stock is perfect for creating a rainbow assortment of books, there are endless other cover options as well. We have made book covers out of calendar pages, digital photos, sheet music, blueprints, scrapbook paper, cereal boxes, corrugated cardboard, and repurposed artwork. They may say you can't judge a book by its cover, but, in my opinion, the jury's still out on that one.

MATERIALS

* card stock (or other creative cover material)
* blank paper
* scissors
* hammer
* nail (or awl)
* string (I use colorful embroidery floss)

* embroidery needle
* decorative labels

How-to

1. Crease the cover paper down the center and then unfold it. Lay the cover face down on a table. Lay blank pages on top of the cover. (If the inside pages are larger than the cover, trim them to fit.) Make a strong crease down the center of the blank pages. Align the cover and blank pages along the center crease.
2. With hammer and nail, make three evenly spaced holes down the center crease.
3. Thread the embroidery floss through a needle. Starting on the outside of the book, push needle and thread through the middle hole to the inside of the book, then out through the bottom hole to the outside, back in through the top hole to the inside, and back out again through the middle hole.
4. Tie a secure knot with the two ends of the floss on the outside of the book. Trim the ends of the string to about two inches long.
5. Close the book, and put a decorative label on the cover for the title and author information.
6. Happy writing!

Variations

For Scribblers: Pre-writers love to fill blank books with, what else? Scribbles! And luckily, all that practice does them a world of good, developmentally speaking.

For Spellers: Emerging writers enjoy making picture books, using drawings or stickers and familiar words.

For Storytellers: Storytellers can fill book after book with bright ideas. Keep a stack at the ready!

For Scholars: Scholars can incorporate elements of real books—such as a title page, a dedication, a table of contents, and an "about the author" page—into their handmade versions.

15

Command Central Message Board

S OME DAYS IT SEEMS as if managing the comings and goings and communications among family members is a job best suited to a highly trained specialist. Part flight commander and part operations engineer, the family manager has to coordinate a multitude of details. The good news is that the same system that works for the most technically advanced agencies also works in our humble homes. I'm talking about creating a command central.

Admittedly low-tech, my version of a good mission control center accomplishes two things: relaying messages and organizing important data. And the best part is, it's so simple that your kids can easily get in on the act. Less micromanaging for you, and more organization for everyone on the team. Oh, and another bonus, there's writing involved too. As they jot down reminders, important dates, or messages, they are making writing-to-remember a daily habit, one that will serve them quite well now *and* in the future.

MATERIALS

* legal-size clipboards (one for each member of the family)
* painter's masking tape
* latex wall paint in a different shade for each family member (I use the little paint samples available in hardware stores; darker colors work better for this project)

* sanded tile grout (about one-half cup)
* paintbrush
* blank labels
* markers
* cup hooks
* chalk

How-to

1. Cover the binder clip on each clipboard with painter's tape.
2. Create your own custom color chalkboard paint by mixing about one tablespoon of sanded tile grout into one-half cup of latex paint. Repeat for each paint color.
3. Paint the board part of each clipboard with the chosen color. Let them dry thoroughly. Remove the painter's tape when the paint is dry.
4. Using blank labels and a marker, label the binder clip on each clipboard with a family member's name.
5. Hang the clipboards on a wall using cup hooks.
6. Leave messages for each family member in chalk on his or her board. Use the binder clip to attach any related, time-sensitive items, like party invitations, event tickets, or driving directions.

Variations

For Scribblers: Post Scribblers' works of art and some notes alongside their clipboard so they know their spot and will be ready to use it when the time comes.

For Spellers: Spellers are just learning to write little notes to family members. The clipboards provide a perfect way for them to distribute all of their correspondence.

For Storytellers: Prolific Storytellers can post their schoolwork and stories at the end of the day for everyone to read and enjoy.

For Scholars: Scholars are well equipped to use the message center to coordinate and communicate life's daily details. For example, they can clip a permission slip to Mom's board and write, "Field trip permission slip due Monday" (which Mom can then sign, clip on the Scholar's board, and write, "Put in backpack; sounds like a great trip!").

16

Say What? Writing Tablet

HAVE YOU EVER LOOKED at your kids and thought to yourself, "What on earth are they *thinking*?" or "What *will* they say next?" Well, ponder no more. Simply help them make a couple of these whimsical tablets, and all your questions will be answered. In writing.

Writing tablets, often used in schools, are a wonderful way for young children to practice writing and to express themselves. At home, we crafted more playful versions of this old-school tool, making one in the shape of a thought bubble and another in the shape of a speech bubble. We borrowed the idea from cartoons and modified it for our own (writing) purposes. And let me assure you, the result is nothing less than some very animated "discussions." Hmmm. What *will* we think of next?

MATERIALS

* poster board
* scissors
* clear contact paper
* dry-erase markers
* paper towel or piece of cloth

How-to

1. Cut a piece of poster board into a thought bubble or a speech bubble shape. (You can easily design your own shapes, or enlarge one of the "Say What? Word and Thought Bubbles" templates on page 209 to the desired size with a copy machine, cut it out, and trace it onto poster board.)
2. Cut a piece of clear contact paper to a size slightly larger than your bubble shape. Slowly peel off the paper backing, and then lay the contact paper, sticky side up, on a table. Carefully place the bubble shape face down onto the contact paper.
3. Trim off excess contact paper by cutting around the edge of the bubble shape.
4. Turn the shape over and smooth out any creases or bubbles.
5. Now show your kids how to write on their bubbles with a dry-erase marker and then erase their musings with a cloth or paper towel.

Variations

For Scribblers: Do you remember Woodstock from the *Peanuts* cartoons? His speech bubble featured a series of dash-like lines that spoke volumes as to his state of mind. Pre-writers' scribbles have the potential to express at least as much.

For Spellers: I can just imagine the words that Spellers will come up with to crystallize their thought processes. To start with, they might use their thought bubble to respond to questions with a silently scrawled "Yes," " No," or "Maybe."

For Storytellers: Bubbling over with ideas already, Storytellers will, most likely, be in a frenzy of writing, erasing, and more writing in order to get it all out.

For Scholars: Scholars will realize that in addition to expressing themselves, they can also express the viewpoints of others (from their own perspective, of course). So watch out, they might try to put some words in your mouth!

17

Scoreboard

KIDS TAKE WRITING WITH THEM, no matter where they go. Even when they're out in the backyard tossing around the ball, writing has a place. To make it official, help them create a backyard scoreboard to keep track of points, wins and losses, and other vital stats.

And while kids may not be writing tons of stuff on their scoreboard, this activity reinforces an important function of writing: keeping track. It helps kids get into the regular habit of pausing the action momentarily to make a note of something, however briefly. It establishes a connection between doing and writing, action and notation. And that's a winning combination, in my book.

The way I see it, it's not whether you win or lose, it's how you *score* the game.

MATERIALS

- * baking sheet
- * chalkboard paint
- * shovel
- * one six-foot-long section of two-by-four lumber (available at hardware stores)
- * drill or screw gun
- * two 1¾-inch wood screws

* one twenty-inch piece of elastic
* old washcloth
* chalk

How-to

1. Paint the baking sheet with chalkboard paint (two to three coats) as directed on the paint can. Allow the paint to dry thoroughly between coats.
2. Select the spot for your scoreboard and dig a hole, two feet deep. Place the wood post in the hole; backfill dirt around the post, and compact it until it feels solid.
3. Drill a small hole in the middle of the baking sheet one and a half inches down from the top, and another hole one and a half inches up from the bottom. Use these holes to screw the baking sheet to the post.
4. Tie elastic tightly around one corner of the washcloth. Tie the other end of the elastic around the post, right below the bottom of the chalkboard. This (along with the rain) is the eraser for your scoreboard.
5. Start keeping score!

Variations

For Scribblers: Scribblers can surely learn to make tally marks. Make it noncompetitive, though. Your suggestion might be, "Put a line on the board every time you catch the ball," and then ask them to see if they can beat their own score the next time around.

For Spellers: Since Spellers are learning to write their numbers, they can keep score numerically, erasing each number or striking it through before writing the next one.

For Storytellers: Storytellers may add some play-by-play descriptions, running commentary, analysis, or predictions to their score-keeping routine.

For Scholars: Scholars can begin to calculate more complex stats, such as batting averages, for example. Becoming proficient in writing numbers quickly, neatly, and in straight lines helps Scholars to focus all their attention on the math (without having to struggle to decode their digits).

18

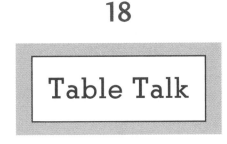

Table Talk

IT'S A CHALKBOARD. It's fabric. No, it's chalk cloth!

What an amazing new material is chalk cloth. I could dream up finicky little projects to do with this stuff all day long. And if you do a search on the Internet, chalk cloth goodness abounds.

But if you prefer projects of the no-sew, no-fuss variety (as many of us do), have I got a good one for you: a chalk cloth tablecloth. The trickiest part is tracking down the chalk cloth (see the resources section at the back of the book). Once you have it, your work is nearly done.

You can toss this tablecloth on the kids' table at holiday parties or on the kitchen table in preparation for a playdate. But don't think it's exclusively for entertaining kids—it's a great teaching tool too. How useful would it be to have a write-and-wipeable tablecloth on the table when your children are doing homework? They can write their math calculations right on the table instead of using scratch paper, figure out how to spell a problematic word, or have a large-scale brainstorming blitz before writing an essay. In fact, any time inspiration strikes your kids in the general proximity of your tabletop, this tablecloth has them covered.

Materials

* measuring tape
* chalk cloth
* scissors
* pinking shears
* chalk
* sponge

How-to

1. First, measure your table. Add ten to fifteen inches to the length to allow for as much overhang as you desire. (Chalk cloth is forty-eight inches wide; if your table is wider than forty-eight inches, then plan on your tablecloth functioning more like a wide table runner.) Use these measurements to figure out the yardage you will need.
2. Cut the chalk cloth according to your measurements. After you have cut it to the intended length and width, trim around all the edges carefully with pinking shears to make a simple yet decorative finished edge that won't fray.
3. Voilà! There you have it. Your final step is to cure the chalk cloth by rubbing it all over with the side of a piece of chalk, up and down and side to side. Repeat this one more time before you wipe it off.
4. You can surface clean your chalk cloth between uses with a damp sponge.

Variations

For Scribblers: Pre-writers love to cover the table with scribbles, squiggles, and doodles. Or show them how to draw a long and winding line that can become a "road" for their toy cars or trains.

For Spellers: Emerging writers will enjoy writing the whole alphabet from A to Z, signing their names, and writing all their favorite words.

For Storytellers: Storytellers will love having the space for a mural-sized drawing *and* a narrative too.

For Scholars: This is the perfect homework helper for Scholars, who will have plenty of room to figure it all out in writing.

19

Scrap Happy

A WRITER'S SCRAPBOOK is a place to collect random bits and-pieces of writing, and any other art and artifacts that help to tell a young writer's story. A scrapbook is like a big, bound collage of writing and the memories that go along with it. It's a playful cut-and-paste collection with serious keepsake potential.

The thing to remember about scrapbooks is that they don't call them "scrap" for nothing. Keep it fun, not fussy. Forgo fancy layouts in favor of letting the scraps speak for themselves. Like a snapshot of a moment in time, a young writer's words require very little embellishment.

Make sure you flip through the scrapbook with your children; it's a perfect opportunity to show them how valued their writing is and how much it has progressed. Looking back inspires young writers to move forward. It inspires them to get working on the next chapter of their life story.

MATERIALS

* blank scrapbook
* writing "scraps"
* photos, drawings, and other memorabilia
* tape
* glue stick

How-to

Together, you and your children can cut, tape, and paste pieces of their writing into a large scrapbook. Include any relevant associated objects, such as photos, drawings, play programs, ticket stubs, or pieces of nature.

Variations

For Scribblers: Put Scribblers' messy masterpieces in the scrapbook in chronological order, and you'll not only have a keepsake, you'll also have a chronicle of an emerging writer.

For Spellers: Save the pages where your Spellers wrote their names for the first time, of course. Tell them how valuable their first signature will be when they're rich and famous one day!

For Storytellers: Oh, the stories. Save as many as you can. You'll be so glad you did!

For Scholars: To document the development of your growing child, include some of the everyday stuff in their writer's scrapbook: a spelling test, a book report, a note to Mom, an IOU to Dad, a letter to Santa, a toy-store shopping list. It's all part of the history of a young writer.

20

Family Tree

A
S WE WERE PREPARING to host a big family Thanksgiving dinner, the subject of relatives came up. In an effort to explain all the branches of our family to my son, I drew a family tree. And although he seemed interested enough, to me the lesson seemed a little, well, flat.

It dawned on me that a family tree should be just that. A family *tree*. From that seed of an idea grew a very meaningful (and beautiful!) activity. We took a break from the busyness to whip up this craft, and boy was I ever glad we did. Our family tree helped us answer some important questions: Are my aunties your sisters? Is my uncle my cousins' father? Is Nanny Daddy's mommy? But more than that, it reminded all of us exactly why we really gather together. (Everything else is just gravy.)

MATERIALS

* a leaf from nature
* piece of lightweight cardboard or card stock
* black marker
* scissors
* one box of natural-colored coffee filters (choose a size slightly
* larger than the size of your leaf)
* red, yellow, and green liquid food coloring

* small paper cups
* brown paper grocery bags
* paintbrush
* marker
* alphabet stampers (optional)
* white glue
* clothespins
* medium-sized bucket or flowerpot

How-to

1. Place a leaf on the cardboard and trace around it with a marker.
2. Cut along the marker line with scissors. This will be your leaf stencil.
3. Trace the leaf shape onto coffee filters using the stencil. Cut out coffee-filter leaves with scissors.
4. Completely cover your work area, as food coloring may stain some fabrics or surfaces. Make homemade watercolor paints by adding eight to ten drops of red food coloring to about one-fourth cup of water in a small cup. Repeat for the yellow and green food coloring, each color in its own separate cup.
5. Spread out the coffee-filter leaves on brown paper grocery bags (or newspaper).
6. Dip your brush in the watercolors and dab paint onto the leaves. You will not need very much paint, as the coffee-filter paper diffuses the liquid throughout the leaf. Continue until all the leaves are colored.
7. Let the leaves dry thoroughly, about thirty to sixty minutes, depending on how much liquid they absorbed.
8. When the leaves are dry, label each with a family member's name, using alphabet stampers or a marker.
9. Crease each leaf vertically down the center. Apply a thin line of glue along the crease and attach the leaf to a clothespin. Let the glue dry.
10. While the leaves are drying, position your tree branch in your flowerpot or bucket. If the tree branch needs to be stabilized

in the container, crumple up some brown paper grocery bags and stuff them in around the base of the branch.

11. When the leaves are dry, your kids can pin them onto the tree. They can take them down, move them around, and arrange them over and over again as often as they wish. Remember, if there is a marriage or a birth in the family, add a new leaf.

12. Keep it up year-round, use it as a seasonal decoration, or bring it out for special family occasions.

Variations

For Scribblers: Pre-writers can cut out pictures of family members and glue them on to their leaves, exercising fine motor skills as they snip and squeeze.

For Spellers: Emerging writers can use alphabet stampers or markers to embellish their leaves with names.

For Storytellers: Storytellers are able to grasp family relationships, and they can arrange leaves accordingly.

For Scholars: Scholars can include some demographic data on their leaves, such as birth date, place of birth, age, place of residence, or occupation.

Do

There's an expression that says: you are what you do. That makes perfect sense to me. It doesn't make much difference who you *think* you are if you don't do anything about it. It's the action that counts. Writing is a perfect example. Who are writers? People who write. Day in and day out, for reasons big and small, people who pick up a pen or pencil to make a list, write a letter, or jot a note are writers.

The daily habit of recording or communicating your thoughts in writing is what defines your role as a writer. When kids learn to make writing one of their written-in-stone daily habits, like reading, brushing their teeth, eating their vegetables, and playing outside, they too are writers. The following group of activities are wonderful no-fuss ways to get writing off of your kids' minds and on to their schedules.

21

Listmania

WHEN SHE WAS LITTLE, my sister Maria wrote about her morning routine:

What I do in the morning:
wake up
p
sharpen my wits
~~watch t.v.~~ eat breakfast
get dressed

I know, priceless. I have the list committed to memory since it's been framed and hanging on the bathroom wall in my parents' house for years. Ahh, the wisdom (and wit) of the young.

There's nothing like lists to put things in perspective. That's their intended purpose, after all. Lists organize, compartmentalize, prioritize. They make life predictable, helping children to anticipate what is coming next (kids *love* that!).

In my humble opinion, they are one of life's most useful tools. And just in case you need more convincing, see my following list of lists.

MATERIALS

* paper
* pencil, marker, or crayon

HOW-TO

The basic gist of the list: number down the left side of the page, and record one important item at a time alongside each number.

Variations

For Scribblers: Parents can write simple to-do lists for Scribblers. Keep lists for the little ones short and sweet—three to four items max. Checkmarks are hard for pre-writers to manage so, true to their name, I usually encourage Scribblers to scribble items out as they complete them.

For Spellers: Show Spellers how to put a box to the left of each number on their list of about four to five simple items, which they write themselves. Then they can check off things as they go.

For Storytellers: Storytellers can handle making their own list, of no more than seven items.

For Scholars: Once children become comfortable using lists as a tool, there are unlimited list possibilities to explore. Check out some list suggestions below.

A LIST OF LISTS

shopping list: things to buy
wish list: things you want someone else to buy for you (please)
to-do list: tasks that you want to get done
honey-do list: tasks that you want someone else to do for you
    (please)
goal list: important things you want to accomplish in the future
play list: songs you want to hear
running lists: frequently updated lists (such as books you want to
    read, shows you want to watch, movies you want to see, places

you want to go, food you want to try, adventures you want to have, people you want to see, or travel destinations)

hot/not list: things that are awesome and things that are so last week

packing list: what to bring

guest list: who to invite

homework list: assignments to complete

forget-me-not list: things to remember

price list: costs of different things

phone list: people to call

22

Places to Go, People to See

WHAT DO MOST super-successful people have in common? An aptitude for creating an agenda.

An agenda is a basic plan of what to do and where to go when. Children crave a schedule because they love to know what is going to happen, both now and later. In fact, the only thing they like better than knowing the schedule is helping to create it. Involve kids in furthering their own agendas, and you'll find that they're eager and willing to put their big plans in writing.

MATERIALS

* paper
* pencil

HOW-TO

1. Put your plans for the day on paper, with your children's help.
2. Encourage your children to consult their agenda periodically, to check off items they've completed and find out what's happening next.

Variations

For Scribblers: Involve pre-writers in creating and following a picture schedule of the day (using basic line drawings or photos) and you'll see that they'll quickly get the hang of the routine.

For Spellers: Using a combination of pictures and words, help Spellers make a schedule on a *big* piece of paper (it will help them get the big picture regarding the passage of time).

For Storytellers: Storytellers can handle making a simple schedule with items numbered to indicate what happens first, second, and so on.

For Scholars: Scholars can go by the clock, making a schedule with times going down the left side of the page and things to do alongside.

23

Daily Journal

EVERYONE SHOULD HAVE a trusted journal, children especially. The word "journal" is derived from the word *jurnee* in Anglo-French. And journaling is indeed a journey, a small voyage of self-discovery we can all take each day.

A journal entry documents the path our day took and our feelings about it. It can be as simple or as in-depth as children choose. Journaling doesn't have to conform to any rules, either; children can express themselves in their journal using colors, drawings, poems, a collage, even a single well-chosen word. The only rule about a journal is to write in it regularly. Before children know it, documenting the day becomes a habit that they can depend on. By taking the time each day to follow where their thoughts are leading them, children gain a clear understanding of not just where they've been, but where they're going as well.

MATERIALS

* blank journal
* pencil
* colored pencils

How-to

In the beginning, the most important thing about a journal is not what a child writes in it, but just that they visit it often. Once journaling becomes a regular habit, the words will most likely follow.

Variations

For Scribblers: Introduce pre-writers to the journaling habit with a "What Color Was Your Day?" journal. Ask children that important question each evening, have them pick one color from an assortment of small-sized colored pencils, and show them how to scribble all over the page with their chosen hue.

For Spellers: Emerging writers respond well to a "Word of the Day" journal. Ask them, "If you could pick any one word, silly or serious, that matches what you were feeling today, what would it be?" The chosen words usually range from peculiar to poignant, and they are always intriguing.

For Storytellers: Help young Storytellers focus with a "High/Low" journal. Prompt them to write something about the high point of their day and something about the low point of their day.

For Scholars: Scholars might find that the words flow more easily when entries are written like a letter to a trusted friend, beginning with "Dear Diary" or "Dear Journal." To emphasize the private nature of their writing, children at this stage often like to embellish their journal with a lock and key. Don't fret. This doesn't mean they're keeping secrets; it just means their thoughts deserve their own personal space. Respect their privacy and resist the urge to peek!

24

Field Guide

ALSO KNOWN AS a nature journal, a field guide documents all the discoveries and adventures children encounter in the great outdoors. Field guide fodder includes thoughts about trees, plants, or flowers; animal observations; weather reports; notes on seasonal changes; and reflections about what's visible in the night sky. Nature-related notations can be brief or may be embellished with details about colors, smells, sounds, and feelings. Journal entries can include simple sketches, and photos or a found object (like a bird feather, fallen leaf, or pressed flower) may be adhered to the page.

A field guide is a place where the wonder of nature and the wonder of writing meet. It's an exercise in seeing the world with eyes wide open, a quality that should certainly be nurtured in young writers.

MATERIALS

* blank notebook or journal
* pencil
* colored pencils, crayons, or markers
* tape
* camera (optional)
* box or basket (optional)

How-to

1. Encourage children to observe nature when they are out and about.
2. When they get home, they can record the details about what they noticed. Or bring their field guides along if your family is headed on a trek or an adventure so they can jot down observations on the go.

Variations

For Scribblers: Pre-writers may start with a nature collection, stored in a box or basket perhaps, with a label attached to each item.

For Spellers: Spellers are ready to start drawing what they see in a notebook when they go for an outing, take a walk, or play in the backyard. They can label their pictures by writing a couple of words, like "baby bird."

For Storytellers: Storytellers are ready to enhance their field guides with more specific observations of the flora, fauna, and fun they observe in nature.

For Scholars: Scholars can include more data such as the location of their observations, time of day, conditions, and any interesting patterns they notice.

25

Travelogue

BEFORE YOU HIT THE ROAD, add one more item to your packing list: a travelogue. You won't regret it. New adventures always spark new insights. And you will definitely be glad you have a place to preserve them all.

When children record their travel reflections they are in good company. Many writers throughout the years have written about their experiences in far-off places. When you read about their trips, their writing transports you. Kids will be able to revisit their own journeys as well when they reread their travelogues. It's like taking a vacation all over again (only without the jet lag).

MATERIALS

- blank notebook, journal, or handmade book
- pencils
- markers
- tape
- glue stick
- shoebox or small suitcase (optional)

How-to

1. As you travel, encourage your children to (briefly) write the names of places they're going, as well as ideas about what they saw and how they felt about it.
2. Kids can also collect bits and pieces along their travels, such as maps, ticket stubs, backstage passes, luggage tags, transportation schedules, receipts, currency, stamps, postcards, and photos.
3. During downtime, kids can embellish their travelogues by cutting and then pasting or taping their found ephemera onto the pages.

Variations

For Scribblers: Pre-writers can store their souvenirs in a shoebox or a small suitcase, and then browse through them when they want to reminisce about their trip.

For Spellers: Snap a picture of Spellers at various locations along your way. They can put these photos in their book and label them "Me at the Grand Canyon" or "Me riding a mule."

For Storytellers: Storytellers can narrate their adventures and add illustrations too.

For Scholars: Scholars can include some scholarly details, such as the history of the places they're visiting, the route you're taking, the daily itinerary, restaurant reviews, and so on.

26

Inventor's Logbook

CHILDREN ARE BORN INVENTORS. Sometimes they even seem to be bubbling over with innovative ideas. Some are hits, some are near misses, and some are even big messes. But no matter what, kids' inventions all share one thing in common: an inspired ability to create something out of nothing.

This irrepressible urge to create is the trademark of an inventor (and the hallmark of a writer). The inventor's logbook is a perfect example of how inventing and writing go hand in hand. Real inventors are required to keep a log of all the ideas and activities leading up to any of their inventions in order to prove that they "own" their creation. Kids can do the same, and, in the process, can claim ownership of all their little ingenious ideas that are just demanding to be documented.

MATERIALS

* graph-paper notebook
* pencil
* colored pencils
* date stamp (available at office supply stores)
* stamp pad
* camera (optional)

How-to

1. Encourage your kids to document their bright ideas in their inventors' logbooks. They can use words, drawings, diagrams, lists, or charts to record their various brainstorms.

2. Show them how to write or stamp the date onto each entry (just for fun, or in case the U.S. Patent and Trademark Office wants to verify their invention's timeline down the road).

Variations

For Scribblers: When your pre-writer does something especially inventive (like using your lint brush to clean up little pieces of dried play dough from the floor), take a picture, date it, and tuck it into a mini album that you can look at together. This will help them get the idea that bright ideas are just begging to be recorded.

For Spellers: Show emerging writers how to draw pictures of their bright ideas, and then label their drawings with arrows and a few words.

For Storytellers: Every inventor wants to be the one to design a better mousetrap. Explain this concept to your Storyteller, see what kind of mousetrap they can come up with, and encourage them to describe their ideas in their logbook.

For Scholars: Scholars may be inspired to design a robot to solve a problem, a widget that makes life easier, or a new and improved version of a familiar gadget. Encourage any and all inventive ideas, and remind them to pull out their logbooks when inspiration strikes. Tell them it's the perfect spot for all of their plans, diagrams, specifications, and instructions.

27

Show-Me-the-Money Ledger

I N ANCIENT TIMES, before the first alphabet was devised, some basic writing systems existed to communicate about one subject in particular: money. You see, even before we had methods of writing our words, we had methods of writing our monetary transactions. First things first, I guess.

Money is serious business, essential to the daily operations of civilized societies. And believe it or not, kids really get this. They understand that the coins in their piggy banks serve a purpose and that it's important to keep track of them. And while they might not be trading their money for a couple of camels and a barrel of grain any time soon, a new toy may be hanging in the balance. (The piggy-bank balance, that is.)

MATERIALS

* blank ledger book
* pencil
* piggy bank (optional)
* money
* calculator

How-to

1. Encourage your children to note financial transactions and goals in their ledger, such as receiving money, spending it, saving for a toy, gifts, or allowance.
2. Show your child how to use the preprinted guidelines in the ledger to line up their writing both horizontally and vertically, making mathematical calculation both easier and more accurate.

Variations

For Scribblers: Pre-writers can begin to learn about money (and work on fine-motor coordination) by doing some simple sorting (making piles of pennies, nickels, quarters, and so on) and counting (e.g., How many pennies do you have?). (Note: for the over-three crowd only, please; coins can be a choking hazard.)

For Spellers: Emerging writers have the ability to count their money, write amounts in their ledger, and perform simple calculations using a calculator.

For Storytellers: Storytellers can include some more information in their ledger about financial goals (saving for a trip to the movies? looking to buy a new toy?).

For Scholars: Entrepreneurial Scholars can actually come up with some ideas to earn money via a small business. Their ledgers will be invaluable to ventures such as creating a lemonade stand, selling handmade goods, or hosting a bake sale.

28

Telephone Messages

H AVE VOICE MAIL, answering machines, and caller ID rendered the good, old-fashioned phone message obsolete? Are message memo pads going the way of the rotary phone? Let's hope not! There's a certain skill involved in relating a phone message. Do you remember playing Telephone, the game, as a kid? One person whispered a message in the ear of the person next to him, and so on and so on, down the line, until the last person announced what she heard. Chances are, by the time it reached the end of the line, the final message bore little resemblance to the original. When kids are challenged to transcribe a phone call, they learn to focus on the most relevant information while filtering out the extraneous stuff. Young writers need to master this kind of information processing to prepare themselves for the rigors of note taking at school, and in life. The more they get to do it, the less that gets lost in translation. Get the message?

MATERIALS

* memo pad, a stack of phone message slips (see "Phone Message Slip" in the templates section on page 210), or a fancy phone message book (available at office supply stores)
* pencil

1. Teach children how to answer the phone and ask relevant questions such as, "May I ask who is calling?" and "May I take a message?"
2. Place a phone message pad alongside a centrally located phone or cordless docking station.
3. Establish a place to leave phone messages where family members can easily find them.

Variations

For Scribblers: Little ones can practice their skills by playing messenger. Have them communicate simple messages from one family member to another (such as, "Please tell your brother that Charlie is coming over to play"). When they can remember one-part messages, challenge them with two-part messages (such as, "Tell him we're having spaghetti for dinner, and it will be ready in ten minutes"). All this practice using their working memory will come in handy when it comes time for writing.

For Spellers: Emerging writers can prepare for real-live message taking by practicing with their pretend phones (or some old cell phones you have saved for play) and a small memo pad. For example, you might ask them to write down the Little League coach's phone number or take a message for Daddy reminding him to fix the leaky sink when he gets home from work.

For Storytellers: Storytellers are ready for some serious lessons (and lots of practice) in phone etiquette. They need to master the give-and-take of conversation in order to listen to and transcribe someone else's words, in between sharing their own little stories.

For Scholars: Your Scholars probably have enough skills by now to run their own switchboard! Take advantage of the opportunity to say, "Hold all my calls!" when you need a break from answering the phone yourself.

29

Autograph Book

This one is really

$$\begin{array}{r} 2\,\text{Good} \\ +\ 2\,\text{Be} \\ \hline 4\,\text{Got 10.} \end{array}$$

SORRY, I COULDN'T HELP IT. The very thought of passing an autograph book around on a momentous occasion makes me all nostalgic.

Not just to be reserved for celebrity signatures, autograph books are a wonderful, writing-filled way to commemorate a milestone. Circulate one at a special event, and everyone can get a chance to write their best wishes, funny quips, and favorite memories. After everyone has signed, the books become keepsakes to cherish. When they're full, sequester them in a safe spot. You and your children will love pulling them out at a later date and poring through all the entries.

MATERIALS

* store-bought or handmade autograph book
* pencil

How-To

Celebrate special occasions by circulating an autograph book and asking everyone to write something special inside. Your children will learn to express their own thoughts by following the example of family and friends. This can become a lovely ritual that may result in some really special written keepsakes.

Variations

For Scribblers: Encourage your Scribbler to "sign" the autograph book by making their own marks on a page, and possibly dictating a thought or two.

For Spellers: Spellers can sign their name in the autograph book and add a couple of words or a drawing.

For Storytellers: Storytellers can write some simple sentiments, silly sayings, a special memory, or a sweet story.

For Scholars: There is a long history behind autograph books, which date back to the fifteenth century. Scholars might get a kick out of doing some simple research to find out if their parents, aunts and uncles, or grandparents remember writing in autograph books as children, and what their favorite entry was.

30

Once Upon a Time

IMAGINATION IS the greatest natural resource of childhood. As luck would have it, it is also one of the most indispensable tools of a writer.

Children are perfectly suited for creating engaging stories, tall tales, and fanciful fiction. Just think about it. They have an amazing sense of wonder; a propensity to think in metaphor; a sensitivity to rhythm, rhyme, and repetition; and an enormous capacity for making things up. In fact, it's actually much easier to teach children how to think like writers than it is to teach seasoned writers to remember how to be as creative as children.

When it comes to spinning a yarn, kids are at a definite advantage. Simply start a sentence with, "Once upon a time . . ." and wait for them to take over. By the time they get to "The end," you'll know exactly what I mean.

MATERIALS

* some favorite books
* paper
* pencil

1. Read a few simple stories with your children and discuss some of the choices the author made. How did the story begin? Who were the characters? Where did it take place? What is the most exciting thing that happened? How did the author wrap up everything in the end?
2. Brainstorm with your children some ideas for stories of their own.
3. When you see their eyes light up about an idea, pull out paper and pencil, and help them get started.

Variations

For Scribblers: Getting pre-writers accustomed to stories couldn't be simpler. Read, read, read. Listening to the rhythm of stories is the best possible prep for them to write stories of their own someday.

For Spellers: Emerging writers get a big kick out of fill-in-the-blank stories. They can make important decisions about the twists and turns of the story, without having to tackle the whole thing all at once (for a sample, see "Fill-in-the-Blank Story" in the templates section on page 211).

For Storytellers: As their name suggests, Storytellers are perfectly suited to this challenge. Just give them a small stack of paper and some loving support, and then admire all the stories they crank out.

For Scholars: Young authors-in-training can begin to consider some of the more technical aspects of writing a story, such as the parts of a story (introduction, body, and conclusion), character development, and setting.

31

Poetic License

I F YOU REALLY WANT to get children's creative writing juices flowing, introduce them to the art of poetry. Poems capture a child's innermost thoughts in a surprisingly eloquent way. Maybe that's because poetry is a little more playful. It tends to dance around the page. It's less linear, more rhythmic, and has fun little patterns to follow. It invites children's brains to think outside the box a bit, and I think they appreciate that.

Writing a poem should be carefree and lighthearted, like skipping instead of walking, eating dessert before dinner, or bursting into song. Tapping into a child's sense of play is not just fun, it's functional as well. When children can relax and enjoy themselves, they are better able to engage both sides of their brain. The creative right side of the brain is activated at the same time the logical left side is, making poetry a whole-brain writing workout. And without even breaking a sweat! Who knew?

MATERIALS

* paper or notebook
* pencil
* colored pencils

How-to

1. First off, read some poetry with your child. (We enjoyed starting with Shel Silverstein and e. e. cummings around here.) Don't do too much explaining at first; try to let the verses speak for themselves.
2. Sit down with your child and write a first poem together, taking turns writing lines. Just see where it goes.
3. Introduce your child to different forms of poetry (some of which are described next), and encourage them to write poems of their own.
4. Have a poetry reading, where your children get to recite their poems out loud in front of the family.

Variations

For Scribblers: Introduce pre-writers to the pattern of poetry by showing them how to make any sort of repeating pattern with their scribbles. Try alternating two colors, lines with curves, or zigzags with loop de loops. This prepares them for some of the rules of poetry they will learn later on.

For Spellers: Spellers are well-suited to trying out what is called an acrostic poem. They choose a significant word, and then write it vertically down the left side of the page, one letter on each line. Then after each letter, they write a word (or words) that begins with that letter, which is also related to their significant word.

M akes me cookies
O odles of kisses
M agnificent

Storytellers: Who doesn't love a haiku? I'm sure Storytellers will. Haikus are three-lined poems featuring seventeen syllables, five in the first line, seven in the second, and five in the third. Something like this:

First of November
Darkness comes much too early
When you're playing ball.

Scholars: Limericks have a distinct rhythm and rhyme (best illustrated by reading out loud) and a propensity for silliness. They're my kind of poem! (Oh, and kids love them too.) I still remember one I wrote in the fourth grade that I was particularly proud of:

> There once was a man from Yonkers
> Who really was quite bonkers
> He loved to dance
> To run and to prance
> And when he fell down he went clonkers.

Need I say more?

Play

Play is the work of kids. Don't let all of that fun fool you. Some serious skill building, learning, and, yes, hard work goes on while children are at play. And do you want to know what's the best part about it? Playful activities are so irresistible, kids don't even know they're educational. (Come to think about it, let's keep that part a secret, just between us.)

It's perfectly okay to let them think it's all fun and games. We know better. We know that some surreptitious setup on our part can go a long way toward making playtime a little more purposeful. We can capitalize on the fact that our kids are at their creative best while at play, by slipping some writing props in among their toys, and suggesting some bright ideas for adding some writing to the playful mix. As a starting point, check out the next group of activities, which feature the perfect blend of function and fun.

32

Priority Mail

PEOPLE ARE CONSTANTLY COMPLAINING about how the price of stamps keeps going up. Me, I don't mind. Call me a throwback, but I have a great deal of appreciation for the USPS. Slip an envelope into a mailbox, and it gets hand-delivered to anyone, anywhere, in the whole country, in mere days. For less than a couple of quarters. Sounds like a bargain to me.

Kids share a similar respect for all things postal. They see a bit of magic when a letter disappears in a mailbox and is received by a faraway friend or relation. And when a response shows up on their own doorstep days later, well, that certainly gets their stamp of approval.

Encourage your kids to have fun with postal pretend play, to pique their interest in future letter writing (which we will discuss in more detail later on). For now, let them be in charge of delivering the goods, whatever they may be. Remember, when you're a kid there's no such thing as junk mail, and every delivery is special.

MATERIALS

* empty postal boxes (or shoeboxes)
* scissors
* junk mail

* paper
* pencils
* postcards
* envelopes
* stamps or stickers
* stampers and ink pad
* postal forms and stickers
* blank labels
* over-the-shoulder bag
* mail carrier dress-up clothes (optional)

How-to

1. Help your kids set up their own personal post office.
2. Turn empty boxes into mailboxes by cutting a narrow opening to slip in letters. You can make one mailbox for each family member, if you choose.
3. Encourage your kids to write some letters. Then they can address, stuff, seal, and stamp the envelopes; use stamps to "postmark" the mail; and fill out postal forms.
4. Kids can play letter carrier by filling up their mailbag and then delivering letters to the right mailbox.

Variations

For Scribblers: You can make some name and address labels for pre-writers to affix to their envelopes. Then they can scribble, stuff, stick, seal, and stamp to their heart's delight.

For Spellers: Let emerging writers play with some large-sized manila envelopes, so they have more space to write the names they know.

For Storytellers: Storytellers can practice folding letters neatly, slipping them in envelopes, sealing them up, and "addressing" them to real or imaginary friends. They may also want to add words and phrases such as, "Special Delivery," "Fragile," "This End Up," "Confidential," "Urgent," or "Return to Sender."

For Scholars: Make a small address book or card file with the names and addresses of Scholars' friends and family. Then teach them the proper positioning of all the information on an envelope. They'll take it from there.

33

The Office

LITTLE KIDS HAVE BIG PLANS. So naturally, they're pretty comfortable with the thought of climbing the corporate ladder, even at a young age. Newbie VIPs quickly get the hang of pushing paper, sorting files, and holding meetings. And need I mention that corporate bigwigs do some big-time writing? Drafting memos, signing paychecks, writing reports, and composing contracts is all in a day's work for young entrepreneurs. In fact, if you set them up with a nice, cushy corporate space (preferably a corner office, with a view), you might just find them minding their own business from nine to five.

MATERIALS

* paper or legal pad
* sticky notes
* index cards
* business cards
* letterhead (see the chapter on "The Write Stuff")
* pens and pencils
* stampers and ink pad
* file folders
* in and out box

* old computer keyboard or laptop
* old telephone or toy phone
* briefcase
* office attire for dress-up: blazers, neckties, high heels, and so on (optional)

How-to

1. To start this play scenario off right, make a nameplate. Think along the lines of "Ms. Smith" or "Mr. Jones" with "The Boss" written underneath.
2. Show kids how to write, shuffle, stamp, sort, file, and otherwise attend to office-related paperwork.

Variations

For Scribblers: Pretend it's your pre-writer's first day on the job. Give them a little orientation to the office, and let them observe you at work to get the idea.

For Spellers: Spellers are particularly fond of signing their names on any and all important documents and of turning index cards into personalized business cards.

For Storytellers: Storytellers are ready to learn about memos. Show them how to fill out the "To:" and "From:" and "Re:" (short for regarding) sections, and they can write important directives from the boss below that (see "Memo" in the templates section on page 212).

For Scholars: In addition to memos, scholarly CEOs can practice writing agendas, meeting minutes, annual reports (don't forget the pie chart!), payroll, budgets, estimates, invoices, brochures, contracts, and pink slips.

34

Private Eye

LIFE IS FULL OF MYSTERIES. Who forgot to put their coffee cup in the sink? Who tracked muddy footprints all over the house? Who took Dad's screwdriver? Where did Mom leave her keys?

Little sleuths are more than willing to track down clues to solve even the most perplexing of puzzles. And how do they manage to remember all the evidence? By writing it down, of course. Whether it's a whodunit or a whathappened or a wherediditgo, pint-sized private eyes can record all the clues in their pocket notepad until the case is closed.

MATERIALS

* flip-top memo pad
* pencil
* magnifying glass
* spy gear: trench coat, hat, sunglasses, newspaper (for hiding behind)

HOW-TO

Show kids how to observe inconspicuously, gather evidence, and hunt for clues. Every lead they find should be written down in their trusty memo pad.

Variations

For Scribblers: Pre-writers can practice looking at things through their magnifying glasses and scribbling in their memo pads when they see something of interest.

For Spellers: With a little direction from you, Spellers can look for some clues, scavenger-hunt style, by checking off items on a checklist.

For Storytellers: Storytellers can jot down clues in their memo pads and make notes about any suspicious behavior they observe.

For Scholars: When there's a real mystery to solve, who ya gonna call? Scholars. When there's an actual problem in need of solving (think: socks going missing in the dryer, a strange unidentified beeping sound, someone or something knocking over your garden gnome), encourage your Scholars to conduct interviews, collect and label evidence, and canvass the witnesses.

35

What's Up Doc?

KIDS LOVE TO PLAY DOCTOR. Helping someone to feel better, whether your patient is a pretending parent or an injured stuffed animal, is empowering. Plus, it's good to be on the other side of the exam table for once. Calling the shots, so to speak.

You may want to point out to your kids that doctors do more than listen to heartbeats, test reflexes, and say, "Open up and say, 'Aaah.'" They also write in patient charts, write prescriptions, and write down care instructions. Mini physicians can do the same when they play doctor. I know every time I get a prescription for "Take two hugs and kisses and call me in the morning," I can't help but feel all better. It's a miracle cure!

MATERIALS

* blank paper or copies of a medical chart template (see "Medical Chart" in the templates section on page 213)
* manila folder
* stapler
* flip-top pad or copies of a prescription template (see "Prescription" in the templates section on page 214)
* scissors
* alphabet stickers or stampers with an ink pad

* large piece of paper
* paper strips (for hospital bracelets)
* tape
* doctor kit (optional)
* doctor dress-up: scrubs, lab coat, mask, rubber gloves (optional)

How-to

1. Help kids make a medical chart by placing a few pages of blank paper (or copies of "Medical Chart" template on page 213) inside a manila file folder, on the right-hand side. Attach the paper using two or three staples along the top edge.
2. Copy and cut out several copies of the prescription template. Turn them into a small pad by stapling them together at the top.
3. Set up doctor's office props and find some patients to examine (friends, siblings, parents, and stuffed animals can usually use some medical care).
4. Encourage your children to observe and examine patients and write their findings and recommendations.

Variations

For Scribblers: Scribblers can create an eye chart for their pretend doctor's office by using fine motor-friendly alphabet stickers or stampers to make letters on a large piece of paper. And while pretending to test vision, they are getting a lesson in letter identification as well.

For Spellers: In addition to writing simple prescriptions, Spellers enjoy making hospital bracelets by writing patient names on thin strips of paper, and then attaching them to their patients' wrists with a piece of tape.

For Storytellers: Storytellers can record basic patient information in a chart, such as height and weight, complaints, and doctor recommendations.

For Scholars: Premed students (I mean Scholars) can record more technical information, such as temperature (expressed in degrees), heartbeat (how many beats per minute, or BPM), and blood pressure (written as a ratio, such as 110/80).

36

Food for Thought

I'S AGE-OLD WRITING ADVICE: write what you know. And what child doesn't know food?

Associating writing with a regular daily activity, like mealtime, is an excellent way for kids to get their writing chops. Since meals happen three times a day, every day, practice is essentially guaranteed. And although you may still insist that you're not a short-order cook, turning the kitchen into a pretend restaurant may seem much more palatable to you when you see how it inspires your kids to write.

Aspiring restaurateurs do a bunch of writing, including:

menus
specials of the day
orders
receipts
shopping lists
recipes
open/closed signs
restroom signs

Whew. That's a lot of writing. Good thing they will have some sustenance to keep them going while they work.

* card stock (for menus and signs)
* flip-top notepad or copies of the guest check template (see "Guest Check" in the templates section on page 215)
* pencil
* markers or crayons
* chalkboard
* chalk
* food and kitchen gadgets (or pretend food and accessories from a play kitchen)
* tablecloth
* potholders
* waiter attire, apron, chef's hat (optional)

HOW-TO

1. Help your children create menus, take orders, and write checks for real and pretend meals.
2. Show your children how to post the specials of the day on a chalkboard or by creating a sign.
3. If your children serve you something particularly delicious, encourage them to write the recipe on a recipe card. (My favorite kid concoction at the moment is sardine soup. Yum!)

Variations

For Scribblers: Scribblers *love* to scribble orders on a flip-top memo pad, just like they see the waiters doing at their favorite restaurant.

For Spellers: Spellers are ready to write simple menus, take orders, fill the orders in their pretend kitchen, and serve them.

For Storytellers: The rituals of fine dining really appeal to Storytellers. They love to dress the part, spread out a tablecloth, set the table, announce the specials, and serve the food with flair.

For Scholars: Scholars can write their own cookbooks, full of the best real, make-believe, or wacky recipes they have created.

37

(Un)Bored Game

THIS IS THE PERFECT ACTIVITY to pull out of your bag of tricks the next time you hear that inevitable lament, "I'm bored." Whether or not your kids appreciate the play on words, suggest that a board game may be the solution. But we're not just talking about any old board game here. We're talking about an unbearably exciting, one-of-a-kind, custom, homemade, DIY board game. Who couldn't help but be enthused by that?

Combine one part creativity with one part competition, stir in some strategy and a lot of luck, whip it all together with some writing, and you get a recipe for an entertaining (and decidedly un-boring) activity.

MATERIALS

* pizza box or large piece of oak tag
* scissors
* markers
* index cards
* small objects or tokens (for game pieces)

How-to Make

1. Cut the top off a pizza box, or use a large piece of oak tag to make a game board.
2. Draw a path around the game board with markers. Indicate places to start and finish. Divide the path up into many small individual squares.
3. Place some obstacles and landmarks around the game board, alongside your path.
4. Write directions on index cards, such as "Move forward three spaces," "Go back five spaces," "Return to Start," "Oops. You're stuck at (name of obstacle)," or "Move ahead to (name of landmark)."

How-to Play

1. Stack all the index cards, writing side down, in a tidy pile and place them next to the game board.
2. Players place their game pieces on the starting spot.
3. Players then take turns choosing a card from the top of the pile and following the directions as written.
4. The first player to reach the finish is the winner.

Variations

For Scribblers: Scribblers will need some help making a simple game board, preferably with a straight path. Using bingo markers, show them how to make game cards by either making one dot or two dots on each card to indicate how many spaces a player should move. The making and playing help develop fine-motor skills and eye-hand coordination. Fun!

For Spellers: Spellers can write one word on each game card, and can move their pieces by spelling the word and moving one spot for each letter.

For Storytellers: Creative Storytellers may enjoy choosing a theme for their games—such as pirate adventure, dinosaur land, or enchanted garden—and writing more detailed (and creative) instructions.

For Scholars: Scholars can create game boards with complex paths, smaller spaces, trickier directions, and more challenging obstacles.

38

Fish Tales

PEOPLE WHO FISH tell great stories, especially about the one that got away. Kids have a knack for telling fish tales too. So naturally, they will love creating their own fishing game and seeing what fun letters, words, and stories they can reel in.

An added benefit of "fishing" for writing ideas is that kids develop their eye-hand coordination while they practice their storytelling skills. And since they're having a blast, they don't realize they're doing it either. The more they play, the better their skills get, and the more likely they'll get hooked. Now that's a game that's definitely a keeper.

MATERIALS

* string
* scissors
* ring-shaped magnet (available in most hardware stores)
* small dowel(s), about twelve inches long
* tape
* card stock or index cards
* hole punch
* paper clips
* markers

(Note: this activity is suited for the over-three crowd only, as magnets and paper clips pose a choking hazard.)

How-to

1. Cut a length of string about eighteen inches long. Tie a ring magnet securely to one end. Wrap the other end of the string around one end of a dowel several times and tie a knot. Secure it with tape.
2. Cut fish shapes, about four inches long, out of the card stock.
3. Punch a hole near the fish's head with a hole punch. Insert a paper clip into each hole.
4. Label each fish with a letter of the alphabet or a word.
5. Place the fish on the floor. Then, have your child hold the dowel fishing pole, with the magnet end of the string hanging down, and try to "catch" a fish.

Variations

For Scribblers: This is an amazing game to play with pre-writers who are just learning letter identification. When they have mastered the whole alphabet, they can fish for the letters in their name.

For Spellers: Spellers can fish for alphabet letters to spell out the words that they know.

For Storytellers: Storytellers are ready to fish for words, and then they can combine their catches to make silly sentences.

For Scholars: Scholars can use this game to fish for letters to spell out spelling words, or they can fish for vocabulary words and define them as they reel them in.

39

Invisible Ink

LEARNING HOW TO SEND secret messages is one of those activities that has a real wow factor for kids. They feel all stealthy when they deliver a blank page to the only confidante who knows the trick to revealing its hidden words. Kids can extend the fun by stashing a message in an envelope marked "Classified," "Top Secret," or "Confidential." They can also deliver a message in a furtive, cloak-and-dagger fashion to heighten the suspense. Just like real secret agents do. (Only without the "This message will self-destruct in ten seconds" warning. That may be somewhat excessive.)

MATERIALS

* water
* baking soda
* small cup
* cotton swabs
* paper
* paintbrush
* purple grape juice (juice from concentrate works best)
* white crayon
* watercolor paint

How-to

1. Make "ink" by mixing one part water and one part baking soda in a small cup.
2. Dip a cotton swab in the mixture and use it to write a secret message on the paper. Let it dry.
3. When you're ready for the message to be revealed, "paint" over it with the grape juice.

Variations

For Scribblers: A nice intro-to-invisible-ink activity for pre-writers is referred to as "crayon resist." Have your little ones scribble all over a piece of white paper with a white crayon. Then they can paint the paper with watercolors and watch their invisible lines appear.

For Spellers: Spellers can stick to writing one or two simple (yet secret) words.

For Storytellers and Scholars: Storytellers and Scholars can write more involved messages.

40

Secret Codes

NOW YOU KNOW your ABCs, but how about your Alpha, Bravo, Charlies?

Secret codes have been used for centuries to relay privileged information. The premise is simple: A symbol, sound, or gesture is used to represent a letter of the alphabet. A key, showing which symbol stands for which letter, is often used to decipher the message.

You can encourage young writers to have fun "writing" messages with alternative alphabets such as the military alphabet, Morse code, nautical flags, or sign language.

Or they can create a secret code of their own by using the secret code worksheet included in the templates section at the back of the book (which becomes the key to figuring out what's what).

MATERIALS

* paper
* pencil
* crayons
* military alphabet, Morse code, or secret code worksheet (see pages 216–218)

How-to

1. Kids can choose a ready-made code and "spell" out a secret message using symbols in place of letters.
2. Or kids can create their own code, by putting a symbol, shape, picture, number, or different letter in each box of the secret code worksheet. When they have filled in the boxes, they can refer to this key when they are writing their messages.
3. Remind kids to give a copy of the key to the message recipients, so their pals can use it to crack the code.

Variations

For Scribblers: Pre-writers can create a pretend code of dots and dashes or *X*s and *O*s arranged in a pattern. Pattern recognition is an important precursor to learning how to spell.

For Spellers: Spellers love to figure out how to write their names using a secret code. Once they master doing this using one code, they can try other codes, or they can encrypt the names of friends and family members.

For Storytellers: Storytellers are ready to write short messages using a code. They will also enjoy decoding messages you (or their secret spy friends) send them in return.

For Scholars: Scholars are ready to make a complex code substituting one letter for another, using numbers to stand for letters, or inventing their own creative glyphs to represent each letter.

41

Fortune-Tellers

WHEN CURIOUS KIDS want to know what fate has in store for them, they let their fingers do the talking. Cheaper than a psychic, handier than a crystal ball, less cryptic than a horoscope, a classic paper fortune-teller tells all. The best part? It's customizable at a whim. Are your kids itching to know if they'll win a million dollars, if their teacher will give a pop quiz, or who will sit next to them on the bus? Tell them to ask the fortune-teller, and they can let their future unfold before their eyes.

(Oh, and by the way, I predict that kids' fine-motor skills will get a workout as well with this one.)

MATERIALS

* paper
* scissors
* pencil
* crayons or colored pencils

How-to Make

1. Start with a standard piece of paper. Take the top right corner and fold it down so that the top edge of the paper lines up exactly with the left-hand side of the paper.
2. Cut off the extra flap of paper on the bottom with scissors to make a square.
3. Unfold the paper and make a crease along the other diagonal. Unfold the paper again (your creases should make an X on the page).
4. Fold each corner of the square down so that they meet in the center of the X. You now have a smaller square.
5. Turn your smaller square over. Fold each corner of the square down, like you did before, so that they meet in the middle again.
6. Write any eight letters of the alphabet on the small triangles you have created around the square. Then lift the triangles up and write eight fortunes, one on each small triangle.
7. After writing the fortunes, fold the flaps back down and crease the square vertically and horizontally.
8. Turn the paper over and write the name of a color on each square (or color each square with a different color crayon).
9. When you're done, slip the thumb and index finger of one hand under two colored squares, and the thumb and index finger of your other hand under the other two. Gently pinch and press all four corners inward, so they meet in the middle.

How-to Play

1. Two players are required: a fortune seeker and a fortune-teller.
2. The fortune seeker chooses a color. The child holding the paper fortune-teller spells out the color while alternately opening and closing the paper fortune-teller in vertical and horizontal directions.
3. Next the fortune seeker chooses a letter. The fortune-teller

opens and closes the paper fortune-teller as they both say all the alphabet letters up to the chosen letter (for, example, if you choose the letter *G,* the fortune-teller would open and close the paper fortune-teller while saying, "*A, B, C, D, E, F, G*").

4. The fortune seeker chooses a final letter. The child holding the paper fortune-teller lifts the flap corresponding to the chosen letter, and then reads the fortune out loud.

5. Good luck!

Variations

For Scribblers: Instead of writing out color names on a square, have your Scribbler scribble each square with a different color crayon.

For Spellers: Spellers can write the letters on the squares, and they will have a blast with all the alpha counting involved.

For Storytellers: Storytellers will enjoy making up elaborate fortunes. Encourage them to be concise and to self-edit in order to fit their big ideas into such a tiny space.

For Scholars: Scholars can show off their sophisticated writing techniques by making the words on the paper fortune-teller ornate, and they can write the fortunes in cursive if they know how.

42

Treasure Hunt

THERE'S NO BETTER WAY to turn a dull day into a delight than by creating an impromptu treasure hunt. Around here, anytime we have something a little special to give someone, we secret it away, and then get to work writing and hiding hints to locate it. The way we look at it, the only thing better than getting an unexpected gift is finding it by following clever clues. Hunting for the booty is irresistibly fun; it's worth its weight in gold!

MATERIALS

* little trinket, treasure, or fun object
* scrap paper
* pencil

HOW-TO

1. The best way to organize a treasure hunt is by working backward. First, hide the treasure.
2. Next, write a clue to lead someone to the spot where the treasure is hidden. Then, hide this clue.
3. Write a clue that leads someone to the spot where you hid the

last clue. Continue hiding and writing clues until you feel you are finished. Hand the last clue you write to the person whom you are sending on the hunt.

Variations

For Scribblers: Pre-writers can get into the treasure hunt spirit (and give their little fingers a workout) by helping to fold up the clues nice and small.

For Spellers: Spellers can write simple, one-word clues, such as "couch," "bed," "bathtub," or "closet."

For Storytellers: Storytellers can write more detailed clues, such as "Go to your bookshelf. Look inside your favorite book."

For Scholars: Scholars can write clues in the form of riddles: "Look behind something soft, fuzzy, and bear-shaped that lives on your bed."

Connect

Quite possibly the coolest thing about writing is its ability to make meaningful connections among people. Think about it. Writing literally has the power to transcend time and space. You can write a letter or send a postcard to people on the other side of the world. You can tell them what you're thinking, even if you can't meet face to face. They can read your words, and then reread them a week from now, a month from now, or a year from now. A conversation is fleeting, but correspondence can be timeless.

Then again, writing is also a wonderful way to connect in the here and now. Slip people a note, and they can hold your thoughts right in the palm of their hands. Near or far, encourage your kids to use their writing skills to build relationships. Use the time-honored favorites in the next section as a guide, and take it from there.

43

Message in a Bottle

MY HUSBAND and I once overheard a man telling some friends about a cruise he had just returned from, during which he visited an "uninhibited island." A slip of the tongue, perhaps, but what a picture it brought to mind!

Writing is full of inhibitions, not the least of which is, "What will people think of what I wrote?" So before children can get comfortable expressing their innermost thoughts, dreams, and wishes to someone they know, sometimes it helps to write to a friend of the imaginary variety first.

Imagine how much easier it is to write down your true feelings when you picture yourself alone on an uninhibited island, writing to a perfect stranger. And although we won't be throwing these bottles into the sea anytime soon (not exactly an environmentally sound choice, these days), you can certainly make a special spot in your children's rooms, for their messages in a bottle. And who knows, maybe one day they'll want to share the contents with you or someone else whom they trust. But until then, keep a lid on it, so to speak. (And maybe tuck some of your secret wishes into a bottle of your own.)

MATERIALS

* paper
* pen

* empty bottle
* bottle cap or cork

How-to

1. Encourage your children to imagine that they are by themselves, on a secret island that no one knows about but them, writing a message to a perfect stranger. Tell them it can contain their innermost feelings, dreams, wishes . . . whatever special thought they might want to preserve for posterity.
2. Show them how to roll up the finished message, and then tuck it into a bottle. Seal the bottle tightly. Ceremoniously place the bottle in a special spot, for their eyes only.

Variations

For Scribblers: Pre-writers can get their feet wet with this activity by practicing at home. Give them scraps of paper and some plastic bottles to tuck their scribbles into.

For Spellers: Spellers might simply want to tuck their name into a bottle, or they might include the names of everyone in the family.

For Storytellers: Storytellers will find this one irresistible. Let their imaginations run wild as they tell their tales, document their dreams, and write their wishes.

For Scholars: Scholars can approach this scientifically, as if the bottle were a time capsule. They might include the date, their geographic location, information about current events, and predictions for the future.

44

Letter Writing

S A CHILD I felt compelled to write letters about almost anything. When my family was planning a trip to the Grand Canyon, I sent a note to the senator of Arizona telling him to expect my arrival. I wrote to the editor of *Time* magazine to object to the computer being named "Man of the Year." And I will never forget my tear-stained letter to the president of the United States that asked, "Why do gerbils have to die?"

When kids have something to say, a letter's a great way to say it. The beauty of a letter is that it allows them the time to compose their thoughts and get to the heart of the matter in a way that a conversation might not. It can also be saved and reread, which makes it even more special.

Letter writing is also a productive means of self-expression. It helps children channel their ideas and emotions in a positive way. Excitement, disagreement, even sadness can be processed on the page. And when kids receive a response to their letter-writing efforts, it makes it sincerely worthwhile.

MATERIALS

* paper, stationery, or letterhead (see the chapter on "The Write Stuff")
* pencil
* envelope

* stamp
* blank labels
* Parts of a Letter sheet (see "Parts of a Letter" in the templates section on page 219)

How-to

1. First show children letter-writing basics, such as starting letters to friends or family with Dear ____, and ending them with Love, ____. What's the best way to teach this? Have them watch you write a letter—to them!
2. When you finish writing your letter, *don't* give it to them! Instead, keep going with the demo. Put the letter in an envelope and seal it, write their name and address on the envelope, add your name and return address, and put on a stamp.
3. Then take a trip together to the mailbox and send the letter on its way.
4. When they finally get their letter, a few days later, it's quite likely they'll be raring to write one of their own. Sit down and write one together!

Variations

For Scribblers: Using blank labels, make stickers with "Dear," "Love," the names of friends and family members, and the children's own names, which they can stick to their various scribbles. They will get a kick out of stuffing the resulting notes in envelopes.

For Spellers: Spellers require only mailing address and return address labels for their envelopes. They can start writing letters on their own.

For Storytellers: Storytellers love to write letters to people real or imagined, whether an out-of-town grandmother or a fairy-tale character.

For Scholars: Scholars are ready to learn the format for the different parts of a letter: heading, greeting, body, closing, and signature (see "Parts of a Letter" in the templates section on page 219).

45

Thank-You Notes

WITH A LITTLE INGENUITY, we can turn the obligatory thank-you note into something much more fun. (Dare I say, even enjoyable?) All it really takes is a slight adjustment in attitude to turn these requisite little expressions of gratitude into something that will actually be gratifying to write.

So how do we breathe new life into the old thank-you note? First of all, we can start by jazzing it up a bit. Make the card out of a repurposed piece of your child's artwork. Or have your children make a drawing of themselves looking immensely happy and grateful, and then make cards out of the drawings by running off a stack of them on the copy machine. Maybe take a picture of your child holding up a big sign that says "Thanks," make multiple copies, and have them write their note on the back.

Next, brainstorm ahead of time some words and expressions that may suitably express their gratitude. "Thank you" is nice, but "You rock!" "You're too cool for school," and "Were you reading my mind?" have a more enthusiastic ring to them.

A little creativity on our part can turn a thankless chore into an exciting reason to write. Try it and see for yourself, and you can thank me later (no note required).

MATERIALS

* creative paper (old artwork, new drawing, photo of your child)
* pencil
* envelopes
* stamps

HOW-TO

Encourage your children to express their gratitude by writing simple thank-you notes. Keep the notes short, sweet, and personal. Make sure your children mention the name of the gift in the note. Don't be tempted to have them write too many at once; it helps to focus on one or two at a time.

Variations

For Scribblers: Write down Scribblers' reactions to questions, such as "How did you feel when you opened the gift?" "What is a super-exciting way to say thank you?" Make sure they get a chance to make their marks on the page as well.

For Spellers: Take some of the pressure off Spellers by helping them complete a fill-in-the-blank style note (see "Thank-You Note" in the templates section on page 220).

For Storytellers: After brainstorming and listing their gift-related emotions, Storytellers will be ready to compose a sensational note.

For Scholars: Challenge Scholars to find some new and improved ways to say thank you. (Like making cards by tracing around a foot, cutting it out, and starting out by saying, "You knock my socks off!") Dare them to come up with something delightfully different (they just may surprise you!).

46

Postcards

WHO SAYS you have to be on vacation to send a postcard? Any time you feel like saying, "Wish you were here" (or "Wish I was there," as the non-vacation version may read), a postcard fits the bill.

Postcards are a simple, carefree way to get kids into the regular habit of correspondence. Just have them write a couple of lines on a card, address it, stick on a stamp, and it's ready to go. They're also super-easy to customize with drawings and photos.

And even better, postcards are the cheapest kind of mail to send (you can get special postcard-rate stamps at the post office). With all the pennies you'll be pinching by sending postcards, maybe you can start saving up for that next vacation. (I got you thinking about it, didn't I?)

MATERIALS

* card stock (or blank, unlined four-by-six-inch index cards)
* postcard template (see "Postcard" in the templates section on page 221)
* scissors
* crayons, markers, colored pencils, stickers, stampers
* pencil
* postcard stamps

* blank address labels
* glue stick

How-to

1. Print the postcard template onto card stock (one side will be blank; the other will be for writing on). Cut it out.
2. Show your children how to put their personal touch on the blank side of a postcard by drawing, coloring, doodling, stamping, or stickering it.
3. On the flip side of the postcard, children can write their message on the left and the recipient's address on the right.
4. Then place a postcard stamp, and it's ready to go. (Repeat for everyone you know!)

Variations

For Scribblers: Pre-writers can scribble on the blank side of a card, and then dictate a short message to you to write on the flip side.

For Spellers: Encourage emerging writers to draw a picture on the blank side of the postcard, and have them write a short sentiment on the flip side. Make some labels with the addresses of friends and family for Spellers to put on their postcards (it will be tricky for them to write the addresses themselves, in such a small space).

For Storytellers: Give Storytellers a contact list of their friends and family member's addresses, a small address book, or a simple card file. Then they can churn out postcards all on their own!

For Scholars: Scholars can learn to turn almost anything into a postcard: photos, pictures from magazines, photocopies of pictures from books, or artwork of their own. They simply need to adhere the postcard very thoroughly to the back of their chosen image with a glue stick, and then let it dry. Then they can write their message, address the postcard, add a stamp, and send it. They'll love finding things that have postcard potential.

47

Passing Notes

I N THIS AGE of text messaging and e-mail, I wonder if passing notes is in danger of becoming a lost art.

I speak from experience on the subject of passing notes. My best friend, Regina, and I dedicated ourselves to perfecting the art of note passing in English class. I dare say we wrote far more notes to be slipped under the desk than we wrote on our papers on top of the desk. It definitely fell under the category of creative writing nonetheless, and isn't that what English class is all about, anyway? (For the record, our teacher didn't agree.)

Instead of encouraging our kids to engage in classroom subterfuge, let's pass along the note-passing tradition in other venues. Notes can be slipped into lunch bags, Mom's laptop bag, or Dad's briefcase, under little sister's pillow, or into the pocket of Grandma's sweater. Pass notes back and forth while passing the time in the waiting room at the doctor's office. Or pass an "Are we there yet?" note around the backseat of the car on a long drive.

Oh, and if you want to help your kids elevate note passing to an art form, teach them how to incorporate some super-fancy note folds. And make sure you demonstrate how to transfer the aforementioned notes discreetly (you never know when the teacher might be looking).

Materials

* paper
* pencil

How-to

Write a note. Less formal than a letter, a note can be about anything that's on your mind. The only requirement is that you keep
it short. Passing notes requires a quick turnaround time, so get
right to the point. One or two sentences max, so your note-passing partner doesn't have to wait too long. It also helps to include a
question, which invites a timely response.

Variations

For Scribblers: Scribblers love to pass along their latest work by slipping
it under a door, for example. Next time they pass you a scribble, add a scribble of your own to their page and pass it back. See how long you can keep the
"conversation" going.

For Spellers: Spellers are ready to start writing some simple notes of
their own, and folding them into small, passable squares.

For Storytellers: Storytellers may enjoy composing a cooperative story
by passing a note back and forth. Every time the note comes back to you, add
a line to the story, and so on, until it's complete.

For Scholars: Scholars will appreciate the opportunity to elevate note
passing to an art form by incorporating a creative note-folding technique,
such as the following:

1. Fold the paper in half the long way, with the writing on the
   inside of the fold. Fold it in half the long way one more time, so
   that you have a long, skinny rectangle.
2. Holding the long rectangle horizontally, fold the bottom left
   corner up to form a triangle on the left edge, and the top right
   corner down to form a triangle on the right edge.
3. Fold the left edge over and in toward the middle again, forming a parallelogram shape. Fold the right edge over and in

toward the middle again, forming a rectangle. Make another diagonal fold at each end, folding the right edge up and folding the left edge down. Your paper should look like an S shape turned on its side.

4. Fold the right side of the S in toward the middle in the front, and then fold the right side back and down.
5. Tuck the left side inside the top of the triangle in back.
6. Now your note is ready for passing!

48

Pen Pal

THERE'S ONE SURE-FIRE WAY for kids to make this great big world seem a little smaller: find themselves pen pals.

Pen pals bridge the gap of geography via good, old-fashioned snail mail. While pen pals share details of their days, each one might also learn about a faraway place or another culture.

A true lesson in diversity, everything about a pen pal's correspondence initially seems different. Different paper, different envelopes, different stamps, different expressions, sometimes even a different language. But the more children write back and forth, the better they learn another important lesson. Among children, and people in general, there are far more similarities than differences. As pen pals become friends, they realize the distance between them is far less than they ever imagined. Which does indeed make it feel like a small world, after all.

MATERIALS

* paper or stationery
* pencil
* envelope
* stamp

How-to

Encourage children to exchange letters with their pen pals on a regular basis—say, every month or so.

Variations

For Scribblers: Scribblers can start by exchanging mail with someone familiar, such as an out-of-town cousin or a grandparent.

For Spellers: Emerging writers will enjoy sending short notes and pictures to a long-distance friend.

For Storytellers: Storytellers can write all about their interests, and ask probing questions to find out what appeals to their pen pals.

For Scholars: Scholars can locate their pen pal's neighborhood on a globe, a map, or via the World Wide Web to learn more information about them and figure out new questions to ask.

49

Greeting Cards

I T USED TO BE relatively easy to pick out a greeting card. There were only a couple of choices, for only the most typical of occasions. Now it's a different story. Greeting cards make music and light up; I'm sure some even dance. They're made for occasions I've never even heard of, and they reflect every possible personal relationship. (I know people who have the knack for finding the most surprisingly appropriate greeting card for any time of the year; think: happy Groundhog Day, from your second-cousin-twice-removed.)

So how come, with all of this hyper-personalization, store-bought greeting cards feel more impersonal than ever? They still share a cookie-cutter quality. Even with all the variety, there's a certain "one size fits all" assumption.

Enter the handmade, handwritten, greeting card. It's certainly more personal than the alternative, and it's a perfect fit every time. While your child's card might not play a tune, they can make it for a song, and it's sure to brighten the day of anyone who is lucky enough to receive it.

MATERIALS

* card stock
* crayons and markers

* stampers and ink pad
* stickers

How-to

Fold the card stock in half. Have your child decorate the outside of the card and write a heartfelt (or funny!) message inside.

Variations

For Scribblers: Pre-writers will enjoy using stampers and stickers to decorate and "write" on their cards.

For Spellers: Help Spellers spell big words like "birthday," "anniversary," and "congratulations," if they ask. The rest they should be able to do on their own.

For Storytellers: Storytellers may want to include a poem, a joke, or a funny little anecdote.

For Scholars: Scholars may want to design a whole collection of cards, one for every special day they can think of. This way, they will have cards at the ready when occasions arise.

50

Party Time

To PARAPHRASE an oldie but goodie: it's their party, and they'll write if they want to. And I assure you, they *will* want to write. Guest lists, invitations, wish lists, seating arrangements, party game ideas—they'll be writing for weeks as they count down to the big day.

Parties are an exciting excuse to put pencil to paper. They involve quite a bit of planning, and kids want to be involved in every last detail. So put them to work!

And believe it or not, it's not all about them. Children actually get almost as excited about throwing a party for someone else. Then there's even more to do: banners to make, cards to create, gifts to tag, cakes to write on with icing. It's education disguised as celebration, and a whole lot of fun!

MATERIALS

* paper
* pencil
* crayon, markers, or colored pencils
* place cards
* gift tags

1. When party (or holiday) planning, a great place to start is with a guest list. Have your children help write a list of the names of everyone they would like to attend.
2. Another ridiculously motivating pre-party writing activity is creating a wish list. Who could resist this one?
3. Have your child contribute to creating and writing invitations a few weeks before the party.
4. As the party approaches, be mindful of all the ways excited children can contribute their ideas through writing.

Variations

For Scribblers: Involve Scribblers in making a giant party banner. Write out the letters of the celebration message in big block letters, and have Scribblers color them in.

For Spellers: Spellers excel at writing names, so definitely delegate writing the guest list, place cards, and gift tags to them.

For Storytellers: Storytellers will delight in making invitations, seating arrangements, and a list of party games and activities.

For Scholars: Scholars can be involved in planning the menu: have them browse through cookbooks, write down their favorite recipes, and help make a list of ingredients.

51

Coupons

WHEN IT COMES to gift giving, children want to know how to make something all by themselves, from start to finish, without having to ask for help. That way, they can maintain the element of surprise.

Enter the coupon booklet. Customizable for any occasion, a cute coupon book is a gift that keeps giving. Show kids how to make their first one, and they'll be able to craft a made-to-order gift for any special occasion or just to show a little everyday appreciation.

Don't be fooled by how easy it looks, though. Children put a tremendous amount of thought into their various offerings. And as economical as it seems, that's an illusion as well. Receive a coupon for "one free anytime hug" or "breakfast in bed with all the fixings" and, no doubt, to you it will be priceless.

MATERIALS

* copies of coupon template (see "Coupon" in the templates section on page 222) or strips of blank paper
* scissors
* colored card stock
* pencil

* crayons, markers, or colored pencils
* stapler

How-to

1. Make several copies of the coupon template and let your kids cut out the coupons.
2. Cut two pieces of colored card stock slightly larger than the coupons. These will be the front and back covers of the coupon booklet. Kids can decorate them with crayons, markers, or colored pencils.
3. Encourage your children to think of a special thing they can do for or with their beneficiary: a favor, a sign of affection, something helpful, a place to go, or time to spend together.
4. When they have all their coupons filled out, show your children how to gather them in a small stack. Then place one piece of card stock on top of the pile and one on the bottom. Staple the whole stack together along the left-hand edge using two to three staples.
5. If, as they say, it's the thought that counts, this gift will be a hit!

Variations

For Scribblers: The only thing that thrills those little Scribblers more than scribbling is doling out hugs and kisses. Show them how to write *X*s and *O*s all over those promissory notes, and enjoy cashing in!

For Spellers: Simplify coupon writing for Spellers by helping them brainstorm a master list at the get-go, so they can refer to it as they write.

For Storytellers: Storytellers will certainly get creative with this one. Encourage them to take a moment before they begin to imagine the giftee in vivid detail, and then envision all the things that would make that person happy.

For Scholars: Scholars can use their coupons to plan an adventure, outing, or event with the recipient, with each coupon representing a part of the plan. Sounds like a win-win kind of gift to me!

52

Love Notes

MY BARELY-FIVE-YEAR-OLD SON couldn't go to bed one night until he wrote "I love you Mom" on a piece of paper. Pajamas on, red crayon in hand, he was doggedly determined. A few mixed-up letters, a couple of crumpled papers, and some help from Daddy later, he handed me his heart on the page. Then, finally, he relaxed enough to fall asleep.

Sometimes, saying how you feel just isn't enough. Spoken words are invisible, untouchable, intangible. Write it down, however, and you can see it, feel it, hold, it, keep it. It's indelible.

Although we may think it, we can't really give someone our heart. But by writing, we can give someone our heart on a page. A love note is a piece of paper that is a little piece of your heart. Teach your child how to write love notes, and I promise you will have many, many happy returns.

MATERIALS

* paper
* writing tool of choice (a red crayon works great!)

How-to

The best way to teach children to write a love note is by example. Write love notes to your children. Often. Put them in lunch boxes, slip them under doors, tape them onto the bathroom mirror, tuck them under your children's pillows. Use a simple, predictable format that is easy for your children to imitate when it comes time for them to write back to you (personalize it according to your child, of course). Try something like the following, for starters.

Dearest _____,
I love you. You are so _____. I love it when we _____ together. You make me _____. I can't wait to _____.
Hugs and kisses,

Variations

For Scribblers: Cut paper into heart shapes and leave it out for Scribblers to discover. When they present you a heart-shaped scribble, ooh and aah over their love note. They'll instantly get the idea.

For Spellers: When my son first started to write, I wrote him a simple note that said "I love you Jack," and I covered it with outer-space stickers. Not only has he kept it ever since, he used it as a model to create roughly a million "I love you Mom" notes. The return on my investment of one minute of time has been unbelievable. With Spellers, sometimes all you have to do is present a model. Then say no more.

For Storytellers: Send Storytellers an "I love you more than . . ." note and see what you get in response. For instance, I might say, "I love you more than a cup of hot tea, a bucket full of daisies, lobster rolls, little red wagons, sunsets, sour cream walnut muffins, cartwheels, and piggyback rides." Then wait and see how you stack up.

For Scholars: As children get older, it is your challenge as a parent to be increasingly subtle in your written displays of affection while remaining relentlessly consistent. What strikes this perfect balance? The lunch box love note. This is your chance every day to show by example how to express feelings in writing. You may not get a written response, but believe me, you are nourishing your young writer with each note. When you show children how natural it is to write about what (and who) you love, you are planting the seeds that will grow into their own lifetime love of writing.

Templates

The following templates can be used to jump-start some of your kids' writing. Simply select whatever templates tickle your fancy, and get writing. Or you can use them as models for creating your own one-of-a-kind writing templates, customized with your own children in mind. Either way, these templates are meant to be a starting point for creative writing. Playful prototypes. I hope they inspire you and your kids to write away.

Please use these templates for your own personal use only. You can photocopy the templates from this book or download PDFs of these templates from www.shambhala.com/TheWriteStart or www.thewritestart.typepad.com.

Anatomy of an Efficient Grasp:
The Dynamic Tripod Grasp

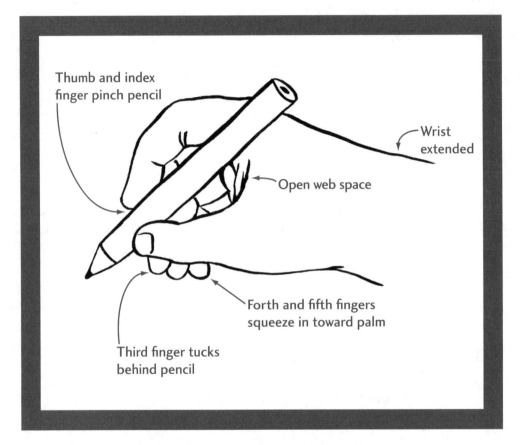

Thumb and index finger pinch pencil

Wrist extended

Open web space

Forth and fifth fingers squeeze in toward palm

Third finger tucks behind pencil

Alphabet Chart

Aa Bb Cc Dd

Ee Ff Gg Hh

Ii Jj Kk Ll

Mm Nn Oo Pp

Qq Rr Ss Tt

Uu Vv Ww

Xx Yy Zz

Cursive Alphabet Chart

Drawing Paper

Article Writing Worksheet

Who?

What?

When?

Where?

Why?

How?

Parts of a Newspaper

The Small Town News

Masthead

Thursday, October 29, 2009   Smalltown, U.S.A.   50 cents

ROCKET LAUNCHES, FINALLY!

Headline

NASA TESTS NEW ROCKET DESIGN

Deck

Dateline

By Jack Mallon — Byline

Cape Canaveral, Florida.
After many delays, NASA cleared their new Ares IX Rocket for takeoff yesterday for a two-minute test flight launched from Kennedy Space Center. The flight, which cost about $445 million, was the first for this newly designed rocket. NASA has been work-ing on the Ares IX for three years. They hope the Ares program will return humans to the moon by the year 2020.

NASA officials called the test flight a success and collected important data that will help them during future flights.

Cutline ➤ The Ares IX, three seconds after liftoff.

Doorknob Sign

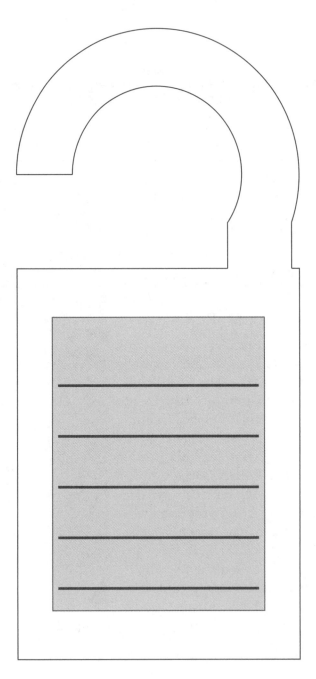

Say What? Word and Thought Bubbles

Phone Message Slip

WHILE YOU WERE OUT:

Name:

Day: Time:

Phone number:

Message:

☐ Called you   ☐ Please call back
☐ Returned your call   ☐ Will call you back later

Message taken by:

Fill-in-the-Blank Story

Once upon a time there was a (circle one) *sweet / mean /
strange /beautiful / brave* _____
who lived in a (circle one) *giant / secret / tiny / enchanted*
_____ near the (circle one) *mountains /
seashore / desert / forest.* One day, at (circle one) *sunrise / sunset /
midnight,* (✓ one) ☐ *he* ☐ *she* met an unusual creature called an

_____.

   ☐ *He* ☐ *She* said to the creature, "_____."
And it replied, "_____."
That was the beginning of a (circle one) *wonderful / shocking /
silly / bizarre* friendship between them, that lasted (circle one)
*forever and ever / for one fun-filled day / for a few memorable
hours.* Together, they liked to (circle one) *play / disagree /
cause mischief / do magic.* Their favorite thing to say was:
"_____."

   They loved to eat (circle one) *delicious / nutritious / fancy /
slimy* _____. When it was time to relax they (circle
one) *sang songs / made up stories / told silly jokes / pondered /
squabbled* about _____.

   Side-by-side they went on amazing adventures to _____.
They made a promise to each other to always _____.
In the end, the two of them lived (circle one) *happily / ridiculously /
unhappily / mysteriously* ever after.

   (✓ one)
☐ THE END
☐ TO BE CONTINUED...

Memo

MEMO

To:

From:

Re:

Status:
☐ Urgent   ☐ Very important   ☐ Nonsense

Medical Chart

Medical Records

Date	Patient Notes

Prescription

NEIGHBORHOOD DOCTOR'S OFFICE

Main Street, U.S.A.

DAW

Refills: _____

☐ None

Signature X _____

Dispense as Written

Guest Check

Guest Check

TABLE	GUESTS	CHECK NUMBER		
	Tax			
Thank You	Total			

Military Alphabet

A:	Alpha
B:	Bravo
C:	Charlie
D:	Delta
E:	Echo
F:	Foxtrot
G:	Golf
H:	Hotel
I:	India
J:	Juliet
K:	Kilo
L:	Lima
M:	Mike
N:	November
O:	Oscar
P:	Papa
Q:	Quebec
R:	Romeo
S:	Sierra
T:	Tango
U:	Uniform
V:	Victor
W:	Whiskey
X:	X-Ray
Y:	Yankee
Z:	Zulu

Morse Code

A · –			1 · – – – –
B – · · ·			2 · · – – –
C – · – ·			3 · · · – –
D – · ·			4 · · · · –
E ·			5 · · · · ·
F · · – ·			6 – · · · ·
G – – ·			7 – – · · ·
H · · · ·			8 – – – · ·
I · ·			9 – – – – ·
J · – – –			0 – – – – –
K – · –			Period · – · – · –
L · – · ·			, – – · · – –
M – –			? · · – – · ·
N – ·			
O – – –			
P · – – ·			
Q – – · –			
R · – ·			
S · · ·			
T –			
U · · –			
V · · · –			
W · – –			
X – · · –			
Y – · – –			
Z – – · ·			

Secret Code Worksheet

A	B	C	D	E	F

G	H	I	J	K	L

M	N	O	P	Q	R

S	T	U	V	W	X

Y	Z	.	,	!	?

Parts of a Letter

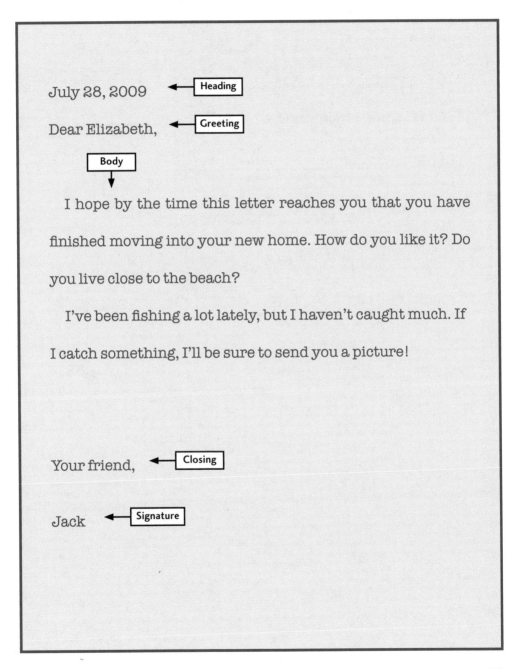

July 28, 2009 ← Heading

Dear Elizabeth, ← Greeting

Body

I hope by the time this letter reaches you that you have finished moving into your new home. How do you like it? Do you live close to the beach?

I've been fishing a lot lately, but I haven't caught much. If I catch something, I'll be sure to send you a picture!

Your friend, ← Closing

Jack ← Signature

Thank-You Note

Dear _____,
(person who gave you the gift)

Thank you very much for the _____.
(name of the gift)

I think it is _____.
(what do you think about the gift?)

I can't wait to _____ with it.
(what do you want to do with it?)

I am _____
(how did you feel when you were given this gift?)

that you were thinking of me.

Love,

_____
(your name)

Postcard

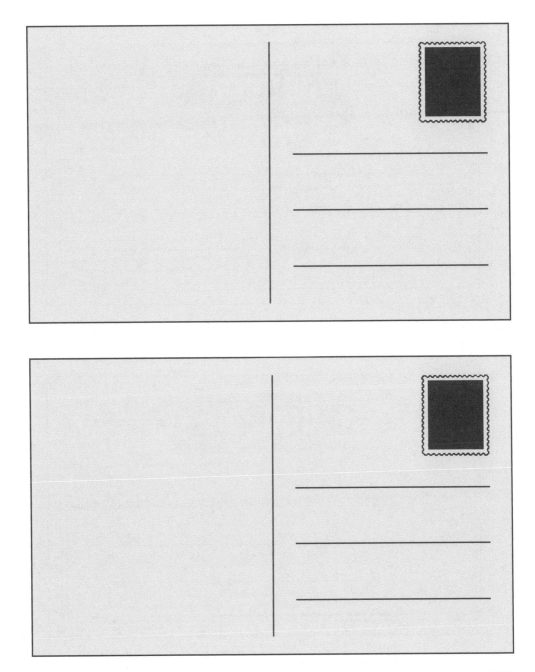

Coupon

Writing Resources

Handwriting Curriculum

Handwriting Without Tears
Developmentally based handwriting tools, resources, workbooks, and an excellent handwriting curriculum, all created by an occupational therapist, Jan Olsen, OTR.
www.hwtears.com

Writing and Art Supplies

General Supplies
www.stubbypencilstudio.com
www.dickblick.com

Chalkboard Paint
www.benjaminmoore.com
www.krylon.com
www.rustoleum.com

Chalkboard Cloth
www.fabric.com
www.nancysnotions.com

Temporary Tattoo Paper
www.beldecal.com

Iron-On Transfer Paper
www.epson.com

Height-Adjustable Desks
www.ikea.com

Educational Supply Stores
www.lakeshorelearning.com
www.discountschoolsupply.com
www.kaplanco.com

Skill-Building Toys and Tools
www.backtobasicstoys.com
www.fatbraintoys.com
www.forsmallhands.com
www.magiccabin.com

Occupational Therapy Tools
www.therapyshoppe.com
www.otideas.com

Self-Publishing Sites

www.blurb.com
www.lulu.com
www.cafepress.com

Photo Book-Making Sites

www.picaboo.com
www.shutterfly.com
www.snapfish.com

Publishing Opportunities for Children

Stone Soup
This international literary magazine, founded in 1973, is published six times a year. Stories, poems, and book reviews are accepted from children eight to thirteen years old.
www.stonesoup.com

Skipping Stones
This multicultural magazine accepts children's original writing in all languages. Five bimonthly issues are published during the school year.
www.skippingstones.org

Anthology of Poetry by Young Americans and *Anthology of Short Stories by Young Americans*
Submissions of poetry and short stories from children in kindergarten through grade twelve are considered for these anthologies, which are published annually.
www.anthologyofpoetry.com

Cricket and related publications *Spider, Ask,* and *Muse*
These magazines have monthly writing contests, each with specific age ranges, themes, and deadlines. Consult a current issue for guidelines.
www.cricketmag.com

Highlights
This magazine publishes children's creative writing, such as poems, jokes, stories, recipes, craft ideas, and book reviews.
www.highlightskids.com

Books for Parents

Games for Writing: Playful Ways to Help Your Child Learn to Write. Peggy Kaye. Farrar, Straus, and Giroux, 1995.

Montessori Read and Write: A Parent's Guide to Literacy for Children. Lynne Lawrence. Three Rivers Press, 1998.

Raising Lifelong Learners: A Parent's Guide. Lucy Calkins with Lydia Bellino. Da Capo Press, 1998.

The Read-Aloud Handbook. Jim Trelease. Penguin, 2006.

About the Author

JENNIFER HALLISSY is a mom and a pediatric occupational therapist who has a happy preoccupation with the art and science of writing development. Having earned her master's degree in occupational therapy from New York University, she teaches courses for parents and professionals. Also a freelance writer, Jennifer contributes to national parenting magazines. She lives in Port Washington, New York, with her husband, Bruce, and two children, Jack (a Speller) and Gracie (a Scribbler). Read along as she explores all things writing-related on her blog, thewritestart.typepad.com.

Index